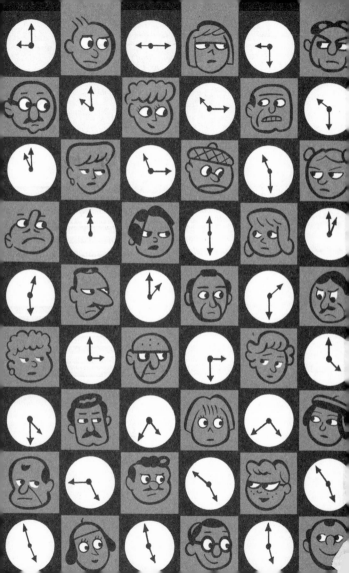

The
WAGE SLAVE'S
GLOSSARY

The
WAGE SLAVE'S
GLOSSARY

BY
JOSHUA GLENN
& MARK KINGWELL

DESIGNED + DECORATED BY SETH

BIBLIOASIS

2011

Glossary © Joshua Glenn, 2011
Introduction © Mark Kingwell, 2011
Illustrations © Seth, 2011

FIRST EDITION

Library and Archives Canada Cataloguing in Publication
Glenn, Joshua, 1967-
    The wage slave's glossary / by Joshua Glenn & Mark
Kingwell ; designed + decorated by Seth.
ISBN 978-1-926845-17-3

    1. Work—Philosophy—Terminology. 2. Work—Social
aspects—Terminology. 3. Work—Philosophy—Humor.
4. Work—Social aspects—Humor. I. Kingwell, Mark, 1963-
II. Seth, 1962- III. Title.

HD4901.G54 2011   306.3'6   C2011-903515-4

Edited by Daniel Wells.

PRINTED AND BOUND IN USA

INTRODUCTION

Wage Slavery, Bullshit, and the Good Infinite

MARK KINGWELL

I ntroducing the volume that precedes the one you now hold, *The Idler's Glossary* (2008), the present author made the following rash claim. "Henceforth all further glossaries are superfluous because *everything you need to know about how to conduct a life* lies within these covers, if only sometimes by implication and omission."

The scholarly qualification at the end of that declaration, meant to be ironic, has instead turned out to be prescient. For another glossary has proved to be necessary; otherwise we would not have brought it into being, and you would not be holding it in your hands right now. So much is obvious. The question that presses on the minds of skeptics and supporters alike is this one: *Why?* Or more precisely: *Who were you kidding the last time, you know, that time you said glossaries were over?*

The answer, dear reader, is not that we were kidding, but that we were too optimistic. *The Idler's Glossary* was intended to expand the vocabularies and minds of dedicated idlers everywhere.

Hinged on the key distinction between *idler* and *slacker*, it sought to defend an idea of life free from the depredations of getting and spending, labour and its sale. The slacker, we noted, is avoiding work; the idler, by contrast, is living according to a scale of value entirely independent of work. The introduction, billed as "the last defence you will ever need," attempted to bolster the glossed words of wisdom with an argument that the idle life was the best life.

We stand by this position, but the assertion about no further defences was, alas, insufficiently grounded. We sent our little book, *The Idler's Glossary*, into the world just as it experienced the biggest economic collapse since the Great Depression. Depending on your degree of irony, that was either foolhardy or excellent timing. Naturally we prefer to think the latter, and to see our modest effort as a sort of retroactive handbook for the heroes of those great 1930s and 40s freedom-from-work Hollywood comedies: Cary Grant and Katharine Hepburn in *Holiday* (d. George Cukor, 1938), or Joel McCrea in *Sullivan's Travels* (d. Preston Sturges, 1942). "I want to find out why I'm working," says the Grant character, a self-made man, in the former film. "It can't be just to pay the bills and pile up more money." His wealthy fiancée – and her blustering banker father, seeing a junior partner in his son-in-law – think it can be just that. Which is why Grant goes off with the carefree older sister, Hepburn, on what might just be a permanent holiday from work. In *Sullivan's Travels*, Hollywood honcho McCrea goes in search of the real America of afflicted life – only to conclude that mindless entertainment is a necessity in hard times. Childlike joy and freedom from drudgery is more, not less, defensible when unemployment rates rise.[1]

---

1 It has been remarked, if not often then at least poignantly, that there has not been, in the wake of 2008's economic meltdown, any sustained political critique of the system or individuals responsible for the collapse. No general strikes. No riots or mass demonstrations. No protest songs, angry novels, or outbreaks of resistant consciousness. In contrast to the Great Depression of the 1930s, the 'recession' or 'correction' or 'setback' (choose your *status quo* euphemism) has barely impinged on the popular media. There are some important exceptions. I will note just three here: Jonathan Dee's novel *The Privileges* (Random House, 2010), a sly satire of the blithe arrogance of one couple who swim through the economic collapse; Chris Lehmann's collection *Rich People Stuff* (OR Books, 2010), which lampoons the favoured tropes and preoccupations of one-percenters; and Roger D. Hodge's angry screed about the Obama Administration's complicity with minimizing the responsibility of Wall Street for the collapse, *The Mendacity of Hope* (Harper, 2010). One complicated example is the hit 2010 film *The Social Network* (d. David Fincher), which tells the story of Facebook 'inventor' Mark Zuckerberg in the unspoken context of the early-2000s bubble. But the film can't decide whether it is a revenge-of-the-nerds celebration or a moralistic slam of internet-age sharp dealing.

The Great Recession of 2008 proved every anti-capitalist critic right. The system was bloated and spectral, borrowing on its borrowing, insuring its insurance, and skimming profit on every transaction. The FIRE sector – finance, insurance, real estate – had created the worst market bubble since the South Sea Company's 1720 collapse and nobody should have been surprised when that latest party balloon of capital burst. And yet everybody was. It was as if a collective delusion had taken hold of the world's seven billion souls, the opposite of group paranoia: an unshakable false belief in the reality of the system. The trouble was that, in the wake of the crisis, awareness of the system's untenability changed nothing. The government bailout schemes – known as stimulus packages, a phrase that belongs easily in the pages of porn – effectively socialized some failing industries, saddling their collapse on taxpayers, even as it handed over billions of dollars to the people responsible for the bloat in the first place. Unemployment swept through vulnerable sectors in waves of layoffs and cutbacks, and 'downturn' became an inarguable excuse for all manner of cost-saving action. Not only did nothing change in the system, the system emerged stronger than ever, now just more tangled in the enforced tax burdens and desperate job-seeking of individuals. Meanwhile, the role of gainful occupation in establishing or maintaining all of (1) biological survival, (2) social position and, especially in American society, (3) personal identity was undiminished.

Capitalism is probably beyond large-scale change, but we should not waste this opportunity to interrogate its most fundamental idea: work. A curious sub-genre of writing washed up on the shore of this crisis, celebrating manual labour and tracing globalized foodstuffs and consumer products back to their origins in toil.[2] The problem with these efforts, despite their charms, is that they do not resist the idea of work in the first instance. The pleasures of craft or intricacies of production have their value; but they are no substitute for resistance. And no matter what the inevitabilists say, resistance to work is not futile. It may not overthrow capitalism, but it does highlight essential things about our predicament – philosophy's job ever.

---

2 See, for example, Matthew Crawford, *Shop Class as Soulcraft* (Penguin, 2009) and Alain de Botton, *The Pleasures and Sorrows of Work* (Pantheon, 2009). Andrew Ross summarizes the political puzzle posed by these books: "It is an unfortunate comment on the generous intellects of these two authors that they do not see fit to acknowledge, in their respective surveys of working life, the nobility of those who resist" ("Love Thy Labor," *Bookforum*, Fall 2009, p. 16).

We should have realized, in short, that our own idle work was not done. For it comes to our attention, again and again since our previous small volume went out into the world, that the values of work are still dominant in far too much of life; indeed, that these values have exercised their own kind of linguistic genius in creating a host of phrases, terms, and labels that bolster, rather than challenge, the dominance of work. Ideology is carried forward effectively by many vehicles, including narrative and language. And we see that this vocabulary of work is itself a kind of Trojan Horse within language, naturalizing and so making invisible some of the very dubious, if not evil, assumptions of the work idea. This is all the more true when economic times are bad, since work then becomes itself a scarce commodity. That makes people anxious, and the anxiety is taken up by work: *Don't fire me! I don't want to be out of work!* Work looms larger than ever, the assumed natural condition whose 'loss' makes the non-working individual by definition a loser.

* * *

We begin by once more acknowledging the great contribution of the philosopher Bertrand Russell to these ideas, even if, as noted in the earlier glossary, he did not get everything right. Russell is in fact more incisive about work than he is about idleness, which he seems to view as the absence of work (in our terms, slacking). Still, in his 1932 essay "In Praise of Idleness," Russell usefully defines work this way:

> Work is of two kinds: first, altering the position of matter at or near the earth's surface relatively to other such matter; second, telling other people to do so. The first kind is unpleasant and ill paid; the second is pleasant and highly paid.

Russell goes on to note that "The second kind is capable of indefinite extension: there are not only those who give orders, but those who give advice as to what orders should be given." This second-order advice is what is meant by *bureaucracy*; and if two opposite kinds of advice are given at the same time, then it is known as *politics*. The skill needed for this last kind of work "is not knowledge of the subjects as to which advice is given, but knowledge of the art of persuasive speaking and writing, i.e. of advertising."

Very little needs to be added to this analysis except to note something crucial which Russell appears to miss: the *greatest work of work* is to disguise its essential nature. The grim ironists of the Third Reich were exceptionally forthright when they fixed the evil, mocking maxim "Arbeit Macht Frei" – work shall make you free – over the gates at Dachau and Auschwitz. We can only conclude that this was their idea of a sick joke, and that their ideological commitments were not with work at all, but with despair and extermination.

The real ideologists of work are never so transparent, nor so wry. But they are clever, because their genius is, in effect, to fix a different maxim over the whole of the world: work is fun! Or, to push the point to its logical conclusion, *it's not work if it doesn't feel like work.* And so celebrated workaholics excuse themselves from what is in fact an addiction, and in the same stroke implicate everyone else for not working hard enough. "Work is the grand cure of all the maladies and miseries that ever beset mankind," said that barrel of fun, Thomas Carlyle. "Nothing is really work unless you would rather be doing something else," added J. M. Barrie, perhaps destabilizing his position on Peter Pan. And even the apparently insouciant Noël Coward argued that "Work is much more fun than fun." Really? Perhaps he meant to say, 'what most people consider fun'. But still. Claims like these just lay literary groundwork for the *Fast Company* work/play manoeuvre of the 1990s or the current, more honest compete-or-die productivity language.

Work deploys a network of techniques and effects that make it seem inevitable and, where possible, pleasurable. Central among these effects is the diffusion of responsibility for the baseline need for work: everyone accepts, because everyone knows, that everyone must have a job. Bosses as much as subordinates are slaves to the larger servo-mechanisms of work, which are spectral and non-localizable. In effect, work is the largest self-regulation system the universe has so far manufactured, subjecting each of us to a generalized panopticon shadow under which we dare not do anything but work, or at least seem to be working, lest we fall prey to an obscure disapproval all the more powerful for being so. The work idea functions in the same manner as a visible surveillance camera, which need not even be hooked up to anything. No, let's go further: there need not even be a camera. Like the prisoners in the perfected version of Bentham's uber-utilitarian jail, workers need no overseer *because they watch themselves.* There is no need for actual guards; when we submit to work, we are guard and guarded at once.[3]

---

3 We could cite, in support here, the analysis of Gilles Deleuze in "Postscript on the Societies of Control," *October* 59 (Winter 1992), pp. 3-7; reprinted in Martin Joughlin, trans., *Negotiations* (Columbia, 1995). Deleuze notes three modes of

Offshoots of this system are somewhat more visible to scrutiny, and so tend to fetch the largest proportion of critical objection. A social theorist will challenge the premises of inevitability in market forces, or wonder whether economic 'laws' are anything more than self-serving generalizations. These forays are important, but they leave the larger inevitabilities of work mostly untouched. In fact, such critical debates tend to reinforce the larger ideological victory of work, because they accept the baseline assumptions of it even in their criticisms. Thus does work neutralize, or indeed

---

social structure: sovereign states (pre-modern); discipline societies (modern); and control societies (postmodern). Whereas a discipline society moulds citizens into subjects through various carceral institutions – schools, armies, prisons, clinics – a control society can be radically decentred and apparently liberated. The difference in the world of work is between a factory and a business. A factory disciplines its subjects by treating them as a body of workers; this also affords the opportunity of organizing and resisting in the form of unionized labour. A business, by contrast, treats employees like hapless contestants on a bizarre, ever-changing game show – something like Japan's "Most Extreme Elimination Challenge," perhaps – where they are mysteriously competing with fellow workers for spectral rewards allocated according to mysterious rules. The affable boss who invites you over for dinner is a paradigm case: Is it business or pleasure? Who else is invited? Does it mean a likely promotion, or nothing at all? Thus does business invade and control the psyche of the worker, precisely because obvious mechanisms of discipline are *absent*.

annex, critical energy from within the system. The slacker is the tragic hero here, a small-scale version of a Greek protagonist. In his mild resistance – long stays in the mailroom, theft of office supplies, forgery of time cards, ostentatious toting of empty files – the slacker cannot help but sustain the system. This is resistance, but of the wrong sort; it really is futile, because the system, whatever its official stance, loves slackers. They embody the work idea in their very objection.[4]

* * *

None of that will be news to anyone who has ever been within the demand-structure of a workplace. What is less clear is why we put up with it, why we don't resist more robustly. As Max Weber noted in his analysis of leadership under capitalism, any ideology must, if it is to succeed, give people reasons to act. It must offer a narrative of identity to those caught within its ambit, other-

---

4 Corinne Maier's otherwise excellent *Bonjour Laziness* (Orion, 2005; trans. Greg Mosse), especially on the language of work, is unstable on this point. She acknowledges the work system is impervious to challenge, and yet finally urges: "rather than a 'new man', be a blob, a leftover, stubbornly resisting the pressure to conform, impervious to manipulation. Become the grain of sand that seizes up the whole machine, the sore thumb" (p. 117). This confused message would seem to indicate insufficient grasp of the slacker/idler distinction.

wise they will not continue to perform, and renew, its reality. As with most truly successful ideologies, the work idea latches on to a very basic feature of human existence: our character as social animals jostling for position. But social critics are precipitate if they argue that all human action was motivated by tiny distinctions between winner and loser. In fact, the recipe for action is that recognition of those differences *plus* some tale of why the differences matter and, ideally, are rooted in the respective personal qualities or 'character' of winner and loser.

No tale can be too fanciful to sustain this outcome. Serbs and Croats may engage in bloody warfare over relatively trivial genetic or geographical difference, provided both sides accept the story of what the difference means. In the case of work, the evident genius lies in reifying what is actually fluid, namely social position and 'elite' status within hierarchies. The most basic material conditions of work – office size and position, number of windows, attractiveness of assistant, cut of suit – are simultaneously the rewards *and* the ongoing indicators of status within this competition. Meanwhile, the competition sustains itself backward via credentialism: that is, the accumulation of degrees and certificates from 'prestigious' schools and universities which, though often substantively unrelated to the work at hand, indicate appropriate elite grooming. These credentialist back-formations confirm the necessary feeling that a status outcome is *earned*, not merely conferred. Position without an attendant narrative of merit would not satisfy the ideological demand for action to seem meaningful.

The result is *entrenched* rather than *circulating* elites. The existence of elites is, in itself, neither easily avoidable nor obviously bad. The so-called Iron Law of Oligarchy states that "every field of human endeavor, every kind of organization, will always be led by a relatively small elite." This oligarchic tendency answers demands for efficiency and direction, but more basically it is agreeable to humans on a socio-evolutionary level. We like elite presence in our undertakings, and tend to fall into line behind it. But the narrative of merit in elite status tends to thwart circulation of elite membership, and encourage the false idea that such status is married to 'intrinsic' qualities of the individual. In reality, the status is a kind of collective delusion, not unlike the one that sustains money, another key narrative of the system.

At this stage, it is possible to formulate 'laws' – actually law-like generalizations – about the structure of a work-idea company, which is any company in thrall to the work idea, including (but not limited to) bureaucracies. Parkinson's, Pournelle's, and Moore's Laws of Bureaucracy may be viewed as derivatives of the Iron Law, understood as ways in which we can articulate how the system sustains itself and its entrenched elite. While expressly about bureaucracies, these generalizations speak to the inescapable bureaucratic element in all workplaces, even those that try to eschew that element. In short, they explicate the work idea even as that idea works to keep its precise contours implicit.

Parkinson's Law is minimalist in concept but wide in application. It states: "There need be little or no relationship between the work to be done and the size of the staff to which it may be assigned." This despite the lip-service often paid to the norm of efficiency. Parkinson also identified two axiomatic underlying forces responsible for the growth in company staff: (1) "An official wants to multiply subordinates, not rivals"; and (2) "Officials make work for each other." The second may be more familiar as the Time-Suck Axiom, which states that all meetings must generate further meetings. And so at a certain threshold we may observe that meetings are, for all intents and purposes, entirely self-generating, like consciousness. They do not need the humans who 'hold' them at all, except to be present during the meeting and not doing anything else.

Examining the company structure at one level higher, that is, in the motivation of the individuals, the science fiction writer Jerry Pournelle proposed a theory he referred to as Pournelle's Iron Law of Bureaucracy. It states that "In any bureaucracy, the people devoted to the benefit of the bureaucracy itself always get in control and those dedicated to the goals the bureaucracy is supposed to accomplish have less and less influence, and sometimes are eliminated entirely." In other words, just as meetings become self-generating, so too does the company structure as a whole. *The company* becomes a norm of its own, conceptually distinct from whatever the company makes, does, or provides.

Once this occurs – most obvious in the notion of 'company loyalty', with the required 'team-building' weekends, ballcaps, golf shirts, and logos – there will be positive incentives for position-seekers to neglect or even ignore other values ostensibly supported by the company. More seriously, if Pournelle's Law is correct, then these position-seekers will become the dominant position-holders, such that any norms outside 'the company' will soon fade and disappear. The company is now a self-sustaining evolutionary entity, with no necessary goals beyond its own continued existence, to which end the desires of individual workers can be smoothly assimilated.

Moore's Laws take the analysis even further. If a bureaucracy is a servo-mechanism, its ability to process an error signal, and so generate corrective commands and drive the system away from error, is a function of the depth of the hierarchy. But instead of streamlining hierarchy and so making error-correction easier, bureaucracies do the opposite: they deepen the hierarchy, adding new error sensors but lessening the system's ability to respond to them. Large bureaucracies are inherently noisy systems whose very efforts to achieve goals makes them noisier. Thus, Moore concludes, (1) large bureaucracies cannot possibly achieve their goals; as a result, (2) they will thrash about, causing damage.

He suggests five further laws. The power wielded by bureaucracies will tend to attach above-mean numbers of sociopaths to their ranks. Hence (3) large bureaucracies are *evil*. Because the mechanism of the system increases noise as it attempts to eliminate it, system members in contact with the rest of reality will be constrained by rigid, though self-defeating rules. Thus (4) large bu-reaucracies are *heartless*. They are also (5) *perverse*, subordinating stated long-term goals to the short-term ambitions of the humans within the system; (6) *immortal*, because their non-achieve-ment of goals makes them constantly replace worn-out human functionaries with new ones; and finally (7) *boundless*, since there is no theoret-ical limit to the increased noise, size, and com-plexity of an unsuccessful system.

* * *

So much for elites looking backward, justifying their place in the work idea, and finding ever novel ways of expanding without succeeding. Pournelle's and Moore's laws highlight how, looking forward, the picture is considerably more unnerving. The routine collection of credentials, promotions, and employee-of-the-month hon-ours in exchange for company loyalty masks a deeper existential conundrum – which is precisely what it is meant to do.

Consider: It is an axiom of status anxiety that the competition for position has no end – save, temporarily, when a scapegoat is found. The scapegoat reaffirms everyone's status, however un-even, because he is beneath all. Hence many work narratives are miniature blame-quests. We come together as a company to fix guilt on one of our number, who is then publicly shamed and expelled. *Jones filed a report filled with errors! Smith placed an absurdly large order and the company is taking a bath!* This makes us all feel better, and enhances our sense of mission, even if it produces nothing other than its own spectacle.

Blame-quests work admirably on their small scale. At larger scales, the narrative task is harder. What is the company for? What does it do? Here, as when a person confronts mortality, we teeter on the abyss. The company doesn't actually do much of anything. It is not for anything important. The restless forward movement of companies – here at Compu-Global-Hyper-Mega-Net, we are always *moving on* – is work's version of the Hegelian Bad Infinite, the meaningless nothing of empty everything. There is no point to what is being done, but it must be done anyway. The boredom of the average worker, especially in a large corporation, is the walking illustration of this meaninglessness. But boredom can lower productivity, so a large part of work's energy is expended in finding ways to palliate the boredom that is the necessary outcome of work in order to raise productivity: a sort of credit-default swap of the soul. Workaholism is the narcotic version of this, executed within the individual himself. The workaholic colonizes his own despair at the perceived emptiness of life – its non-productivity – by filling it in with work.[5]

It can be no surprise that the most searching critic of work, Karl Marx, perceived this Hegelian abyss at the heart of all paid employment. But Marx's theory of alienated labour, according to which our efforts and eventually our selves become commodities bought and sold for profit to others, is just one note in a sustained chorus of opposition and resistance to work. "Never work," the Situationist Guy Debord commanded, articulating the baseline of opposition. Another Situationist slogan, the famous graffito of May 1968, reminded us that the order and hardness of the urban infrastructure masked a playful, open-ended sense of possibility that was even more fundamental: *Sous les pavés, la plage!* Under the paving stones, the beach!

Between Marx and Debord lies the great, neglected Georges Sorel, a counter-enlightenment and even counter-cultural voice whose influence

---

5 More extreme measures can be imagined. In J. G. Ballard's novel *Super-Cannes* (2000), bored executives at a sleek French corporate park are advised by a company psychiatrist that the solution to their lowered output is not psychotherapy but psychopathology: once they begin nocturnal sorties of violence on immigrant workers and prostitutes, productivity rates soar.

can be seen to run into the likes of Debord, Franz Fanon, and Che Guevara; but also Timothy Leary, Jack Kerouac, and Ken Kesey. Like many other radical critics, Sorel perceived the emptiness of the liberal promise of freedom once it becomes bound up with regimentation and bourgeoisification of everyday life. Sorel was a serial enthusiast, moving restlessly from cause to cause: a socialist, a Dreyfusard, an ascetic, an anti-Dreyfusard. In the first part of the twentieth century he settled on the labour movement as his home and proposed a general strike that would (in the words of Isaiah Berlin, who had tremendous respect for this against-the-grain thinker):

> call for the total overthrow of the entire abominable world of calculation, profit and loss, the treatment of human beings and their powers as commodities, as material for bureaucratic manipulation, the world of illusory consensus and social harmony, or economic and sociological experts no matter what master they serve, who treat men as subjects of statistical calculations, malleable "human material," forgetting that behind such statistics there are living human beings.[6]

---

6 Isaiah Berlin, *Against the Current: Essays in the History of Ideas* (Hogarth Press, 1979), p. 320.

In other words, late capitalism and all that it entails.

We might wonder, first, why such resistance is recurrently necessary but also, second, why it seems ever to fail. The answer lies in the evolutionary fact of *language upgrade*. In common with all ideologies, the work idea understands that that victory is best which is achieved soonest, ideally before the processes of conscious thought are allowed to function. And so it is here that language emerges as the clear field of battle. Language acquisition is crucial to our evolutionary success because it aids highly complex coordination of action. But that same success hinges also on the misdirection, deception, control, and happy illusion carried out by language, because these too make for coordinated action. Thus the upgrade is at the same time a downgrade: language allows us to distinguish between appearance and reality, but it also allows some of us to persuade others that appearances are realities. If there were no distinction, this would not matter; indeed, it would not be possible. Deception can only work if there is such a thing as truth, as Socrates demonstrated in the first book of Plato's *Republic*.

Jargon, slogans, euphemisms and terms of art are all weapons in the upgrade/downgrade tradition. We might class them together under the technical term *bullshit*, as analyzed by philosopher Harry Frankfurt. The routine refusal to speak with regard to the truth is called bullshit because evasion of normativity produces a kind of ordure, a dissemination of garbage, the scattering of shit. This is why, as Frankfurt reminds us, bullshit is far more threatening, and politically evil, than lying. The bullshitter "does not reject the authority of the truth, as the liar does, and oppose himself to it. He pays no attention to it at all. By virtue of this, bullshit is the greater enemy of the truth than lies are."[7]

Work language is full of bullshit, and hence so are the pages that follow. But by glossing these terms rather than using them, we hope to bring the enemy into fuller light, to expose the erasure that work's version of Newspeak forever seeks. Special vigilance is needed because the second-order victory of work bullshit is that, in addition to having no regard for the truth, it passes itself off as innocuous or even beneficial. Especially in clever hands, the controlling elements of work are repackaged as liberatory, counter-cultural, subver-

---

7 See Harry Frankfurt, *On Bullshit* (Princeton University Press, 2005), a huge international bestseller which was in fact a repurposed version of a journal article Frankfurt had published many years earlier, included in his collection *The Importance of What We Care About: Philosophical Essays* (Cambridge, 1988).

sive: you're a skatepunk rebel because you work seventy hours a week beta-testing videogames. This, we might say, is meta-bullshit. And so far from what philosophers might assert, or wish, this meta-bullshit and not truth is the norm governing most coordinated human activity under conditions of capital markets. Thus does bullshit meet, and become, filthy lucre; and of course, vice versa.

As the work idea spins itself out in language, we observe a series of linked paradoxes in the world of work: imprisonment via inclusion; denigration via celebration; obfuscation via explanation; conformity via distinction; failure via success; obedience via freedom; authority via breezy coolness. The manager is positioned as an 'intellectual', a 'visionary', even a 'genius'. 'Creatives' are warehoused and petted. Demographics are labelled, products are categorized. Catchphrases, acronyms, proverbs, clichés, and sports metaphors are marshalled and deployed. Diffusion of sense through needless complexity, diffusion of responsibility through passive constructions, and elaborate celebration of minor achievements mark the language of work.

And so: Outsourcing. Repositioning. Downsizing. Rebranding. Work the mission statement. Push the envelope. Think outside the box. Stay in the loop. See the forest *and* the trees. Note sagely that where there is smoke there is also fire. Casual Fridays! Smartwork! Hotdesking! The whole nine yards! Touchdown! You-topia!

These shopworn work-idea locutions have already been exposed, and mocked, such that we may think we know our enemy all too well. But the upgrade/downgrade is infinitely inventive. Even this glossary cannot be considered the final word on wage-slave verbiage. If *The Idler's Glossary* naively declared glossaries over, the present volume warns that the work of language-care is never over.

* * *

You might think, at this point, that a language problem naturally calls for a language solution. The very same inventiveness that marks the ideology of work can be met with a wry, subversive counter-intelligence. Witness such portmanteau pun words as 'slacktivism' or 'crackberry' which mock, respectively, people who think that forwarding emails is a form of political action and those who are in thrall to text messages the way some people are addicted to crack cocaine. Or observe the high linguistic style of office-bound protagonists from Nicholson Baker's *The Mezzanine* (1988) and Douglas Coupland's *Generation X* (1991) to Joshua

Ferriss's *Then We Came to the End* (2007) and Ed Park's *Personal Days* (2008).

These books are hilarious, and laughter is always a release. But their humour is a sign of doom, not liberation. The 'veal-fattening pen' label applied to those carpet-sided cubicles of the open-form office (Coupland) does nothing to change the facts of the office. Nor does calling office-mateyness an 'air family' (Coupland again) make the false camaraderie any less spectral. Coupland was especially inventive and dry in his generation of neologisms, but reading a bare list of them shows the hollow heart of dread beneath the humour.[8] Indeed, the laughs render the facts more palatable by mixing diversion into the scene of domination – a willing capitulation, consumed under the false sign of resistance. This applies to most of what we call slacking, a verb at least as old as 1530, when Jehan Palsgrave asked of a task-shirking friend "Whye slacke you your busynesse thus?"

That was the main reason we were at pains to distinguish idling from slacking in the previous glossary. Slacking is consistent with the work idea; it does not subvert it, merely gives in by means of evasion. As John Kenneth Galbraith pointed out a half-

---

8 See, for example, http://www.scn.org/~jonny/genx.html.

century ago in *The Affluent Society* (1958), such evasion is actually the pinnacle of corporate life:

> Indeed it is possible that the ancient art of evading work has been carried in our time to its highest level of sophistication, not to say elegance. One should not suppose that it is an accomplishment of any particular class, occupation, or profession. Apart from the universities where its practice has the standing of a scholarly rite, the art of genteel and elaborately concealed idleness may well reach its highest development in the upper executive reaches of the modern corporation.

Galbraith's 'idleness' is not to be confused with genuine idling, of course; the 'concealed' that modifies his use of the word shows why. A slacking executive is no better, and also no worse, than the lowliest clerk hiding in the mailroom to avoid a meeting. But neither is idling, which calls for openness and joy.

And so here we confront again the Bad Infinite at the heart of work. What is it for? To produce desired goods and services. But these goods and services are, increasingly, the ones needed to maintain the system itself. The product of the work system is work, and spectres such as 'profit' and 'growth' are covers for the disheartening fact that, in Galbraith's words, "[a]s a society becomes increasingly affluent, wants are increasingly created by the process by which they are satisfied." Which is only to echo Marcuse's and Arendt's well-known aperçus that the basic creation of capitalism is *superfluity*[9] – with the additional insight that capitalism must then create the demand to take up such superfluity. Galbraith nails the contradiction at the heart of things: "But the case cannot stand if it is the process of satisfying wants that creates the wants. For then the individual who urges the importance of production to satisfy the wants is precisely in the position of the onlooker who applauds the efforts of the squirrel to keep abreast of the wheel that is propelled by his own efforts."[10]

---

9 Arendt famously distinguishes *work*, *labour*, and *action* – the three aspects of the *vita activa* – in her magnum opus, *The Human Condition* (1958). In this schema, labour operates to maintain the necessities of life (food, shelter, clothing) and is unceasing; work fashions specific things or ends, and so is finite; and action is public display of the self in visible doings. Work as we are discussing it in the present essay is obscurely spread across these categories. As a result, Arendt could indict the emptiness of a society free from labour – the wasteland of consumer desire – but could not see how smoothly the work idea would fold itself back into that wasteland in the form of workaholism.

---

10 Compare a more recent version of the argument, in the nihilistic words of the Invisible Committee, a group of radical French activists who published their anti-manifesto, *The Com-*

Still, all is not lost. There is a treasure buried in the excess that the world of work is constantly generating: that is, a growing awareness of a *gift economy* that always operates beneath, or beyond, the exchange economy. Any market economy is a failed attempt to distribute goods and services exactly where they are needed or desired, as and when they are needed and desired. That's all markets are, despite the pathological excrescences that lately attach to them: derivatives funds, advertising, shopping-as-leisure. If we had a perfect market, idling would be the norm, not the exception, because distribution would be frictionless. As Marcuse saw decades ago, most work is the result of inefficiency, not genuine need. This is all the

---

ing Insurrection, in 2009 (anon. English trans., Semiotext(e)): "Here lies the present paradox: work has totally triumphed over all other ways of existing, at the same time as workers have become superfluous. Gains in productivity, outsourcing, mechanization, automated and digital production have so progressed that they have almost reduced to zero the quantity of living labor necessary in the manufacture of any product. We are living the paradox of a society of workers without work, where entertainment, consumption and leisure only underscore the lack from which they are supposed to distract us" (p. 46).

It is perhaps no surprise that the authors, viewing this superfluous majority as set off against the self-colonizing desires for "advancement" in the compliant minority, suggest that the current situation "introduces the risk that, in its idleness, [the majority] will set about sabotaging the machine" (p. 48).

more true in a FIRE-storm economy. Paradoxically, idling is entirely consistent with capitalism's own internal logic, which implies, even if it never realizes, the end of capitalism. This insight turns the Bad Infinite of work into a Good Infinite, where we may begin to see things not as resources, ourselves not as consumers, and the world as a site not of work but of play.

The great Marxist and Situationist critics of work hoped that critical theory – accurate analysis of the system's pathologies – would change the system. The latest crisis in capitalism has shown that it will not. But a system is made of individuals, just as a market is composed of individual choices and transactions. Don't change the system, change your life. Debord's "Never work" did not go far enough. Truly understand the nature of work and its language, and you may never even think of work again!

THE WAGE SLAVE'S GLOSSARY

For Susan Roe

The Wage Slave's Glossary

JOSHUA GLENN

99ERS A colloquialism of recent vintage describing out-of-work Americans who have exhausted their unemployment benefits. The moniker refers to the 2009 American Recovery and Reinvestment Act, which allowed many unemployed citizens to receive up to 99 weeks of unemployment insurance benefits. Rush Limbaugh, among other conservative pundits, was not sympathetic: "Extended unemployment benefits do nothing but incentivize people not to look for work." See: BENEFITS (EMPLOYEE), UNEMPLOYMENT

ABSENTEEISM The practice of staying away from work for no one specific reason. Formerly considered a breach of an implicit contract between trusting employer and untrustworthy employee, today *absenteeism* is often regarded as an indicator of psychological, medical, or social maladjustment to work. Psychologists tell us that absenteeism is best understood via the "withdrawal model," which is to say that frequently absent individuals are withdrawing from dissatisfying work. See: MONDAY (SAINT), WORK AVERSION DISORDER

 ADMIN *Admin* (administration) consists of the performance or management of business operations – which sounds innocent enough. However, in the Preface to a 1961 edition of his *Screwtape Letters*, which depicts the ethos of Hell as eerily similar to that of a bureaucratic corporation, novelist C.S. Lewis laments, "I live in the Managerial Age, in a world of 'Admin.' The greatest evil is not now done in those sordid 'dens of crime' that Dickens loved to paint. It is not done even in concentration camps and labour camps. In those we see its final result. But it is conceived and ordered (moved, seconded, carried, and minuted) in clean, carpeted, warmed and well-lighted offices, by quiet men with white collars and cut fingernails and smooth-shaven cheeks who do not need to raise their voices." See: BUREAUCRACY

 AFTER-DINNER MAN In the early 17th century, a man who returned to his place of work after dinner was to be pitied; either the *after-dinner man* was overly devoted to labor, or else

he had too much of it. Today, who *doesn't* open the laptop of an evening – instead of spending time with family and friends, or reading, meditating, playing the ukulele – in order to answer work emails for a while, or put final touches on a Power-Point report? We are all after-dinner men and women, now. See: OFFICING, TELECOMMUTING

AFTERNOON FARMER A 19th-c. slang term for one who wastes time all morning rather than busying himself with proper work. Today, thanks in no small part to online social networking, workers waste time not only in the morning but *all day long*. When downsizing consultants query Peter Gibbons (Ron Livingston) about his routine in Mike Judge's 1999 comedy *Office Space*, Gibbons explains: "Well, I generally come in at least fifteen minutes late [...] and, uh, after that I just sorta space out for about an hour... I do that for probably another hour after lunch, too. In a given week I probably only do about fifteen minutes of real, actual, work." See: PLAYBOR, SLACKOISIE

AIR FAMILY A snarky phrase, from Douglas Coupland's 1991 novel, *Generation X*, referring to the false sense of community experienced by co-workers in an office environment – but those days are over. In the British and US versions of the mockumentary TV series *The Office*, managers David Brent and Michael Scott are the only characters deluded enough to confuse their colleagues with family. See: CLOVIS, OFFICE SPOUSE

 ALIENATION Marxist theory explains that *alienation* is a systematic result of wage slavery. Deprived of the opportunity to conceive of themselves as authors of their own destinies, deciders of their own actions, and owners/users of the value created by their work, workers in a capitalist social order are alienated from: the work they produce; from working itself (which, in a factory setting, tends to be an interminable sequence of repetitive, trivial, and meaningless motions – as parodied by Charlie Chaplin and Lucille Ball); from themselves as producers (an important aspect of human nature, or "species-being"); and from each other. See: ASSEMBLY LINE, CAPITALISM, WAGE SLAVERY

AMBITION We can carbon date the end of the old-skool hip hop era (approx. 1974-83) by studying the genre's lyrics for evidence that the early spirit of light-hearted competition between hip hop acts has been replaced by (a) politically engaged new-school hip hop, about which this *Glossary* has

nothing but praise; and (b) commercially lucrative gangsta rap, whose celebration of crime, drugs, violence, and misogyny might be explained away as a confrontational act of artistic ventriloquism, but whose glorification of materialistic *ambition* cannot be forgiven. A line from 2Pac's 1996 song "All Eyez on Me" captures the spirit of hip hop's new era: "Dangerous and ambitious, while schemin' on gettin' riches." See: CAREERISM, GRAVY TRAIN

 ANT-IFICATION A 2006 British neologism described households in which adult children live with their parents and all work toward group financial goals as *ant-hill families*. And a professor at the University of International Business and Economics in Beijing has approvingly referred to industrious young Chinese college graduates, who live in cramped conditions on the outskirts of cities, as the *ant tribe*. When did we decide that we ought to behave more like ants? Hasn't anybody seen *Them*? See: BEE (BUSY AS A)

ANTI-SABBATICAL Though it was published in 1991, Douglas Coupland's *Generation X* is an Eighties novel. Back then, college grads could afford to take

a job with the intention of staying only for a year. The point of doing so, Coupland notes in coining this term, is "to raise enough funds to partake in another, more personally meaningful activity such as watercolor sketching in Crete." Can today's résumé-padding high-schoolers and undergrads relate to this bygone ideal? See: MCJOB

ANTI-WORK ETHIC Philosophers and social critics from Paul Lafargue (*The Right to Be Lazy*) and Bertrand Russell (*In Praise of Idleness*) to Ivan Illich (*The Right to Useful Unemployment*) and Bob Black (*The Abolition of Work*) have agreed that because labor tends to cause unhappiness, society should be organized in such a way as to lessen the quantity of labor. Hear, hear! Please note, though, that the arguments against working too much advanced in Timothy Ferriss's recent bestseller, *The 4-Hour Workweek*, are far more limited and selfish than, say, Ivan Illich's. See: *The Idler's Glossary*

ASSEMBLY LINE An efficient but alienating manufacturing process, popularized by the Ford Motor Company between 1908 and 1915, in which interchangeable parts are added to a product in a sequential manner. René Clair's 1931 film *À nous la liberté* depicts working conditions in an industrial factory that produces record players as being similar to those in a prison workshop. The scene in which Émile (Henri Marchand) absentmindedly disrupts the *assembly line* likely influenced the hilarious yet sobering opening scene of Chaplin's *Modern Times*. See: ALIENATION, FORDISM

ASSEMBLY-LINE HYSTERIA In 1978, when female employees informed the management at the Silicon Valley semiconductor manufacturer Signetics about aches, dizziness, and confusion caused by noxious fumes on the shop floor, company officials maintained that this was nothing but "assembly-line hysteria." Only after male employees came forward with similar concerns did the company finally investigate. See: ASSEMBLY LINE

ASSIDUOUS The secret to success, or so they told us at my high school, is "applying ass to chair." So why aren't those of us who are *assiduous* [from the Latin for "sitting down to"], which is to say unwearyingly diligent in our sit-down work, treated with the same sentimental respect as are those laborers whose toil requires them to remain standing? Sitting down all day can be trying, even tortuous work! See: STAKHANOVITE

ATTENTION (CONTINUOUS PARTIAL) Multitasking is motivated by an imperative (i.e., to get more accomplished) that, though misguided, is not entirely indefensible. But one possible negative consequence of multitasking is *Continuous Partial Attention*, a disorder first diagnosed in the mid-2000s. It's the overworked office worker's version of Post-Traumatic Stress Disorder, with which syndrome it shares certain symptoms: e.g., always feeling tense and jumpy, inability to focus on anything. See: LEISURE SICKNESS, MULTITASKING

 AUTOGESTION This French term is considered untranslatable – though it is often translated, anyway, as "workers' self-management," or "workers' control." Such phrases limit *autogestion* to the factory, but in 1960s France it first began as a social movement revolting against the abuses of hierarchy, a technique of democratic management, a rejection of the organization of the state, a new doctrine of social experimentation in which power is exercised at the lowest possible level (the factory, but also the street, the classroom, etc.), and an altruistic worldview emphasizing the need for changes in relationships between individuals. See: AUTONOMISM, PROUDHONISM

AUTONOMISM Marxist organizers attempt to ameliorate or revolutionize a capitalist social order via the state, trade unions, and political parties; but since the 1960s in some Western and Southern European countries, proponents of *autonomism* [from the Greek for "living by one's own rules"] have emphasized an everyday, bottom-up resistance to capitalism. Strategies of this "post-Marxist" resistance movement have included: absenteeism, slow working, squatting, and do-it-yourselfism. The movement's anthem is, or ought to be, Bow Wow Wow's danceable anti-work-ethic single "W.O.R.K. (N.O. Nah No No My Daddy Don't)" from 1981. See: AUTOGESTION, DIY

BALL THE JACK Though it would become mostly popular among railroad workers, the origin of this 1910s US slang expression – usually taken to mean "work hard and speedily" – remains mysterious. However, its use in a 1913 jazz song of that title ("Step around the floor kind of nice and light/ Then you twis' around and twis' around with all your might/ Stretch your lovin' arms straight out in space/ Then do the Eagle Rock with style and grace/ Swing your foot way 'round then bring it back/ Now that's what I call 'Ballin' the Jack'") suggests that the expression really means "to work so hard and speedily that you pass into a frenzied trance." See: GRAFT, GRIND

BANDH Derived from a Hindi word meaning "closed," *bandh* is a general strike used by activists in India, Nepal, and elsewhere to protest unpopular government decisions. Shops are expected to stay closed, buses and cabs to stay off the streets. The *bandh* is descended from the *hartal*, an anti-British general strike frequently organized by Gandhi during the days of British colonial rule in India. See: BOSSNAPPING, GHERAO, STRIKE

BANDWIDTH At least since the mid-twentieth century, workers have borrowed terminology related to the machines that they operate in order to describe their own sadly mechanized routines. During the 1990s, analog metaphors (e.g., *downtime*) began to give way to digital ones, such as *blowing the buffer* and *multitasking*, both of which were coined to describe a computer's capacity to manage many tasks at once. A computer's *bandwidth* is the amount of data that can be passed along a communications channel in a given period of time. Next time a colleague complains that he's lacking bandwidth, tell him he needs a "fatter connection." See: DOWNTIME, FORDISM

BANYAN DAY This obscure mid-18th-c. British sailors' expression was first used to describe any day onboard during which meat wasn't served to the crew; the term *Banyan* was inspired by a caste of Hindu merchants in the East Indies who ate no meat one day a week. By the 19th century, though, the meaning of the term had shifted. According to *The 1811 Dictionary of the Vulgar Tongue*, it meant Saturday, or any day of the week without work – and thus without money to eat. See: LOAF-DAY, SATURDAY

BARNACLE Wobbly lingo meaning "a fellow who sticks to one job for a year or more." The term was doubtlessly inspired by that tenacious arthropod of the same name.
See: WOBBLIES

BBS Workplace *behavior-based safety* programs shift responsibility for on-the-job injuries from employers to workers. The BBS movement originated in the 1930s when Herbert William Heinrich, who worked for Traveler's Insurance Company, reviewed supervisor-written accident reports and concluded that most accidents, illnesses, and injuries in the workplace are directly attributable not to, let's say, hazardous conditions or procedures, but to "man-failures," i.e., the unsafe actions of workers. Taking their cue from behavioral psychology, BBS programs since then have attempted to influence the behavior of workers rather than prioritize the improvement of workplace safety conditions (materials, machines, procedures). Meanwhile, due to a lack of adequate whistle-blower protections, those workers who report hazards or make claims are often threatened with discipline. See: CIP, KAIZEN

BEACH BUM We've inherited from European Romantics like Paul Gauguin the conviction (as expressed, e.g., in 1968 Situationist slogans, Elvis movies, and *Baywatch*) that real life – which is occluded from our everyday view – is a beach. But we've also inherited a stern counter-narrative that insists the beach is where man comes to ruin. Recall, for example, that 1967 episode of *The Andy Griffith Show* in which Howard, Mayberry's town clerk and intellectual manqué, boldly drops out of society only to discover that Americans (including one played by the haggard Harry Dean Stanton) who relocate to the Caribbean are pathetic lost souls. To be a *beach bum*, according to this influential meme, is to fail even at dropping out. See: BURNOUT, CLAMBAKE

BEAN-FEAST or BEANO An annual feast once given by employers to their workers. In *The Ragged Trousered Philanthropists*, a 1914 classic of British working-class literature written by a house painter, the titular "philanthropists" are laborers who acquiesce in their own exploitation. Not only do they throw themselves into backbreaking labor for mean wages, they also pitch in funds for their own *beano*. They spend weeks planning it (though they're unwilling to spend one minute listening to socialist agitators); and at the feast they're exhorted by their boss to work harder. See: WAYZ-GOOSE, WORK (WELFARE)

 BEE (BUSY AS A) Bees work tirelessly, without ever taking orders or varying their routines, only to be unceremoniously shoved out of the hive when they become useless to the collective. Yet in his 1994 book, *Out of Control*, Kevin Kelly sings the praises of "swarm systems," i.e., hive-like collections of autonomous members. Steven Berlin Johnson waxes enthusiastic, in his 2001 book *Emergence*, about the similarities between sophisticated recommendation engines and nature's adaptive self-organizing systems – like, say, a beehive. Although these technofuturists' enthusiasm for "control without authority" is infectious, surely we mustn't regard the neo-totalitarian beehive as a model of or for the Good Life. See: ANT-IFICATION, YAKUZA

BENEFITS (EMPLOYEE) It doesn't seem outrageous to describe leisure time, sick leave, and disability income as basic human rights; and there's an argument to be made for including healthcare, social security, and even profit sharing on that list. Yet in our topsy-turvy society they're considered *employee benefits*. They are quantitatively but not qualitatively different from perks, like allowances for lunch or discounted tickets to Disney World! Note: A *benefits slave* is someone who can't leave her job because she can't afford to take one that doesn't offer the same benefits. See: JOB LOCK, PERKS

 BENEFITS (UNEMPLOYMENT) Payments made, as part of a larger social security or social welfare scheme, to unemployed people – with the exception, in the US, of part-time, temporary, and self-employed workers, not to mention workers who were not laid off but fired. Note that in Canada, until 1996 the system now known as Employment Insurance was known as Unemployment Insurance; the name was changed due to negative connotations. In England, unemployment insurance is formally known as Jobseeker's Allowance, and informally as *the dole* (or, in Scotland, *the broo*). So are unemployment benefits a handout or a stimulus? Ask your representative. See: UNEMPLOYMENT

BFOQ/BFOR In US and Canadian employment law, employers are allowed to consider certain qualities or attributes – which, if considered in other contexts, would constitute discrimination – when making decisions on the hiring and retention of employees. One example of such a *bona fide occupational qualification* (*requirement*, in Canada) is the mandatory retirement age for airline pilots. Sounds OK, but the restaurant chain Hooters recently claimed, upon being sued by the US Equal Employment Opportunity Commission, that exuding female sexuality counts as a bona fide occupational qualification. After Hooters agreed to hire some token ugly, hairy members of the male sex as bartenders, the EEOC backed down. See: DISCRIMINATION (EMPLOYMENT)

BLACKBERRY PRAYER Coined by an anonymous workplace wag in the late 2000s, this snarky phrase refers to the oddly supplicative posture characteristic of distracted white-collar types – seated around a conference table, say – who, instead of paying attention to the meeting at hand, are indiscreetly fiddling with their Blackberries. See: MICROBOREDOM

BLACKLEG *Blackleg* predates *scab* as a pejorative moniker (among unionized miners) for a strikebreaker. In the late 1960s, the militant 19th-c. Northumberland folk song, "Blackleg Miner," which warns "They grab his duds and his pick as well,/ And they hoy them down the pit of hell./ Doon ye go, and fare ye well,/ You dirty blackleg miner!", was rediscovered by labor-friendly folk singers. See: SCAB, UNION (TRADE OR LABOR)

BOREOUT Management-theory-speak meaning "a syndrome of emotional exhaustion and disillusionment caused by office work that is underwhelming and unsatisfying." In an effort to cope, office workers draw out tasks so that they take much longer than necessary, then spend the rest of week goofing off. This has been going on since long before the term *boreout* was coined. In the 19th century, Thomas Love Peacock, a longtime employee of the British East India Company, wrote: "From one to two, found nothing to do;/ From two to three began to foresee/ That from three to four would be a damned bore." See: JOB ENLARGEMENT, TEDIUM

BOSS A 17th-c. British workmen's slang term adapted from *werkbaas*, the Dutch word for "foreman, overseer." By the 19th century in England and the United States, the term *boss* was being used, without sarcasm, in white-collar settings – thus demonstrating that office workers had become every bit as servile as any brutalized drudge on a Dutch colonial plantation. ("I had to return, make an awkward apology to boss," complains Washington Irving in an 1806 letter, "and look like a nincompoop.") NB: the jazz slang term *boss-man* is an ironic one. See: MANAGER, PLANTATION

 BOSSNAPPING A form of lock-in where employees detain management in the workplace. The term gained wide usage in 2009, after French employees at a factory owned by US manufacturer 3M held the plant manager hostage for nearly two days in a labor dispute over layoffs. Earlier that year, the head of Sony's French operations was held hostage overnight by angry employees, protesting the terms of the severance package for workers who had been laid off; and workers at a Michelin factory held two managers hostage overnight. PS: The CBS reality show *Undercover Boss* is a kind of twisted, middlebrow version of this phenomenon. See: GHERAO, STRIKE

BRACERO PROGRAM From 1942 through 1964, the series of laws and diplomatic agreements known as the *Bracero Program* – from the Mexican term *bracero*, manual laborer – allowed temporary contract workers from Mexico to work in the US. The program mandated that employers maintain a certain level of wages, housing, food, and medical care for the workers. In 1948, when migrant workers en route back to Mexico died in a plane crash, Woody Guthrie wrote "Deportee (Plane Wreck at Los Gatos)," his last great poem/song. After the program ended, the United Farm Workers under César Chávez would transform migrant labor. See: MAQUILADORA PROGRAM

BRADFORD FORMULA In the 1980s, at the Bradford University School of Management, British researchers using factorial analysis developed a formula that highlights the disproportionate level of disruption on an organization's performance that can be caused by frequent incidences of short-term absence (i.e., absenteeism) when compared with single incidences of long-term absence. Ten instances of absences, each of one day, this formula would have us believe, is one hundred times more disruptive than one instance of absence with a duration of ten days. See: ABSENTEEISM, TAYLORISM

 BRAINSTORMING In the 1920s, the Surrealists invented various parlor games to challenge bourgeois certainties; one of these, a group creativity technique designed to generate a large number of ideas for the solution of a problem, was dubbed *brainstorming*. The bourgeoisie weren't slow to discover a profitable application for the game: in the '40s and '50s, Alex Osborn, cofounder of the now-huge ad agency BBDO, published bestsellers like *Your Creative Power* and *Applied Imagination*, which showed how groups could increase their creative output via brainstorming. NB: Researchers have found no evidence of the technique's effectiveness for enhancing either quantity or quality of ideas generated. See: OFFICE (LIFESTYLE)

BREADWINNER The member of a household who earns all or most of the income. In W. Somerset Maugham's cynical 1931 play of that title, the staid

61

stockbroker Charles Battle decides to relieve his boredom by leaving his trivial wife and entitled children and migrating to the colonies where he can work for his own benefit. In 2010, *BusinessWeek* ran a trend story on a new "reluctant breadwinner" trend: women who wanted to stay home until their income suddenly became critical (e.g., because their husbands were laid off) to the well-being of their families. See: BEACH BUM, INCOME

 BREAK A period of time during a work shift in which an employee is permitted to take time off. Despite the informal, relaxed sound of the term, meal, restroom, and even smoking *breaks* are regulated by law and closely monitored by employers. "Tea up!" says Bertha (Vida Hope), upon hearing their factory's tea signal, to Sidney Stratton (Alec Guinness) in the 1951 anti-wage-slavery comedy, *The Man in the White Suit*. "Tea?" says Stratton. "No thanks, I think I'd rather..." Bertha rudely interrupts: "Tea break! We had to fight for it." Ah, such a charming ritual. See: GUOLAOSI, LUNCH HOUR

BREAK (COFFEE) In office-supply stores everywhere you can purchase industrial-sized canisters

of coffee. Why is this foodstuff sold in the same manner as, say, laser-printer toner? Because for mechanized workers, coffee is fuel. A number of hip hop artists warn against the allure of the *coffee break*: "People get hired/Drink coffee to stay wired/ So they don't get tired, sleep late, and get fired" raps Canibus on "Shove This Jay-Oh-Bee." The rapper Aesop Rock's 2001 anti-wage slavery album, *Labor Days*, contains the sad couplet "I'll be waking with the best of the routine caffeine team players/ for the cycle of it"; and his 2007 song "Coffee" castigates the caffeinated worker who has become a "marionette who will clap and obey." See: FORDISM, ROBOT

BRIGHTSIZING Corporate downsizing in which those workers with the least seniority – i.e., those more recently recruited workers who are often (though not always) younger, better trained and more highly educated – are let go. Also known as *dumbsizing*. See: DOWNSIZING, GREYBEARDING

BROUGH SOWERBY According to *The Meaning of Liff*, Douglas Adams' 1983 dictionary of things that there aren't any words for yet, this invented phrase describes "One who has been working at that same desk in the same office for fifteen years and has very much his own ideas about why he is

continually passed over for promotion." See:
PETER PRINCIPLE

BROWN-NOSE To behave obsequiously, curry favor with a manager or boss. The term is originally US military slang; if you don't understand its scatological origin, try using your imagination. Related terms include: *apple polisher*, *ass kisser*, *bootlicker*, *sycophant*, *toady*, and *truckler*. See: CAN-DO, EMPLOYEE OF THE MONTH

BUFFLING A portmanteau neologism composed of "business" and "waffling," to *buffle* means "to incessantly use corporate jargon, such as 'thinking outside the box,' 'touch base,' 'at the end of the day,' 'going forward,' 'blue-sky thinking,' 'proactive,' 'brainstorming,' 'pushing the envelope,' or 'in the loop,' in a non-work setting." See: BRAINSTORMING, PRIGUISTICS

BUREAUCRACY The sociologist Max Weber claimed that the modern *bureaucracy* evolved from feudalist administrative structures with a few key changes. Whereas the structure of traditional authority is diffuse, in a bureaucracy authority is organized hierarchically; the rules in traditional authority are always subject to change, while in a bureaucracy they're inflexible; officials in a traditional structure can be dismissed arbitrarily, while in a bureaucracy they enjoy tenure of position and look forward to life-long careers. Together, these seemingly rational qualities of the modern bureaucracy have helped bring about a perverse social order that resembles ancient Egypt, Weber wrote, except that it is built on "technically more perfect, more rationalized, and therefore much more mechanized foundations." See: ADMIN, INTERNSHIP

BURNOUT Coined in the 1970s by psychologists in the free clinic movement, the term *burnout* means "long-term mental and emotional exhaustion and a reduced sense of personal accomplishment." Workers who score highest on the Maslach Burnout Inventory (which asks questions like, "Do you feel that you do not have time to do many of the things that are important to doing a good quality job?" and "Do you feel that you are in the wrong organization or the wrong profession?") tend to include doctors, teachers, and emergency service workers. See: BOREOUT, JOB SATISFACTION

CAN-DO It should come as little surprise to hear that one of the earliest published examples of the colloquialism *can do* appears in a 1903 story by...

Rudyard Kipling, whom George Orwell and others have criticized as a propagandist for duty-bound, gung-ho militarism and nationalism. "Four hundred and twenty knots," commands a commander, in Kipling's story. "Can do," replies his underling, with a slangy terseness that almost obscures his obsequiousness. See: BROWN-NOSE, EMPLOYEE OF THE MONTH

CAPITALISM The source of capitalist profits, we read in Marx's writings, is the unpaid effort of wage laborers, who start out with two strikes against them: they don't own the means of production, and they produce more value than they're compensated for. The workers' employers (who own the means of production) use the worker-created surplus value to buy more means of production. Because they have not yet achieved class consciousness, the exploited workers have no idea that the condition of *capitalism* is reproduced by... themselves. Strike three! See: ALIENATION, WAGE LABOR

CAREER In the 16th century, this term [from the Latin for "wagon-road"] meant "circular race-course"; in the 17th, it meant a "rapid and continuous course of action." By the early 18th century, *career* had come to mean "a person's progress through that period of life during which they are primarily engaged in remunerative work." During the 20th century, the notion of a career-as-progress was widely debated: too often, one's career felt like a circular racecourse around which one rushed without ever achieving anything meaningful either collectively or individually. These days, thanks in part to a low level of job security, the term instead means something like "a lifelong process consisting of many work experiences." See: JOB PRECARIOUSNESS, RAT RACE

CAREER GIRL or WOMAN As portrayed in popular culture at mid-century, according to Lynn Peril's 2011 history, *Swimming in the Steno Pool*, career girls were "bouncy, kicky young things who spent their lunch hours shopping for new clothes that would appeal to both boss and boyfriend." Working with an eye not to marriage but promotion and the ultimate goal of a corner office, Peril recounts, marked an individual as a *career woman*, which is to say, a masculinized ice queen. "Most of them are driving and driven women, lonely and vulnerable, leading dissatisfied and empty lives," actress Rosalind Russell, star of *His Girl Friday*, snarkily announced. See: MOM BOMB, PROFESSIONALISM

CAREER GUIDANCE Social reformers pioneered *career guidance* (or counseling) in the early 20th century. In 1958, America's National Defense of Education Act endorsed a close relationship between aptitude testing and career guidance; half a century later, though, many regard guidance counselors as worse than useless. In the movie *Office Space*, for example, Peter (Ron Livingston) says, "Our high school guidance counselor used to ask us what you'd do if you had a million dollars and you didn't have to work.... I never had an answer. I guess that's why I'm working at Initech." His coworker Michael (David Herman) replies: "No, you're working at Initech because that question is bullshit to begin with. If everyone listened to her, there'd be no janitors, because no one would clean shit up if they had a million dollars." See: CAREER

CAREER OPPORTUNITIES "They offered me the office, offered me the shop/ They said I'd better take anything they'd got," growls Joe Strummer on the first Clash album. "Do you wanna make tea at the BBC?/ Do you wanna be, do you really wanna be a cop?" See: MCJOB

CAREERISM The pursuit of professional advancement and power through any positive or negative nonperformance-based activity (i.e., activities in which an employee can manipulate her superiors) deemed necessary, and doing so at the expense of one's personal life and ethics. Part of this definition is lifted from a 2004 Human Resources Development book titled *The Dark Side of Organizational Behavior*, the authors of which praise *impression management* in the workplace, but warn that it can turn into *extreme careerism*. If you ask me, they're splitting hairs. See: BROWN-NOSING

CHAINSAW CONSULTANT In the 1990s, turnaround specialist Albert J. Dunlap counseled CEOs to make widespread cuts in their business operations, including massive layoffs and plant closings, in order to streamline operations, thereby making money (in the short term, anyway) for the businesses' shareholders. Doing so made him very rich, and won him the moniker "Chainsaw Al," hence this more general moniker. See: DOWNSIZING

CIP A theory of management – the acronym stands for *continuous improvement process* – in which, by viewing manufacturing as a holistic system and making ongoing, incremental improvements to its processes, a business increases quality while reducing costs. In the 1940s and '50s the American statistician W. Edwards Deming taught statistical process control (SPC) methods to wartime production workers and later to Japanese businesses. Deming endeared himself to Japan by contributing to its industrial rebirth; he should perhaps also be popular among workers everywhere because of his insistence that "The worker is not the problem. The problem is at the top! Management!" See: EFFICIENCY, KAIZEN

CITIZEN'S DIVIDEND Thomas Paine's 1797 pamphlet *Agrarian Justice* advocates a form of social security: i.e., a universal old-age and disability pension, as well as a fixed sum to be paid to all citizens on reaching maturity. Whence would come the revenue for this *citizen's dividend* (as the proposed state policy was later dubbed)? Because the natural world is the common property of all persons, the state would raise the revenue for a citizen's dividend by leasing or selling natural resources – which, today, is believed to include the electromagnetic spectrum; and the industrial use of air, e.g., carbon dioxide production. See: INCOME

CLAMBAKE "I've got this feeling to be free/ I pick and choose the life I want/ And that's the life for me/ Clambake, gonna have a clambake...." Are the lyrics from this catchy anthem to anti-alienation (sung by Elvis Presley in the 1967 movie *Clambake*) crypto-Marxist? One can't help but suspect that they are, particularly after viewing the scene in that movie in which Elvis organizes six Miami Beach cuties into an assembly line and then dances atop a speedboat while they varnish it. See: ALIENATION, BEACH BUM

CLOCKLESS WORKER Corporate jargon for an employee who doesn't leave her job behind at 5 p.m. because she has internalized management's "clockless" definition of the workday. By extension, it refers to any can-do or brown-nosing employee seeking to demonstrate that management's concerns are her own. See: CAN-DO, CAREERISM

CLOVIS "One who actually looks forward to putting up the Christmas decorations in the office," according to Douglas Adams' 1983 definition of this original coinage. See: AIR FAMILY

COLLAR (BLUE or WHITE) The etymology of the terms *blue-collar* and *white-collar* is too obvious to relate. More interesting is what "blue-collar" has come to mean in a post-industrial era; instead of signifying "working-class," the adjective signifies "hard-working, and proud of it." Thus, a million-aire football player can be described as "blue-collar," while the guy at the register at McDonald's is considered a white-collar worker! See: CAPITALISM

COLLAR (OUT OF) Out-of-work 18th-c. flunkies described themselves as being *out of collar* – a variation, probably, of the workhorse-related phrase "out of harness." Being out of collar isn't a bad thing, necessarily: "Run away from all your boredom," instructs the Placebo song "Slave to the Wage." "Run away from all your whoredom and wave/ Your worries and cares goodbye." See: HORSE, NOSEBAG (PUT ON THE)

COMMUTING The term dates to the 1840s, when businessmen who rode the streetcar or train from the suburbs (now known as "commuter belts") into the city would pay a "commuted" fare. Today, the average American drives 51 minutes to and from work. ("And if your train's on time/ You can get to work by nine/ And start your slaving job to get your pay" – "Takin' Care of Business," by Bachman-Turner Overdrive.) Economists at the University of Zurich tell us that people with long daily journeys tend to overvalue the material fruits of their commute (e.g., money, house in the suburbs, prestige) and to undervalue the goods they're giving up: e.g., sleep, exercise, fun. In this regard, *commuting* strongly resembles smoking. See: FLEXECUTIVE

CORPORATE VALUES Thanks to management gurus Tom Peters and Bob Waterman, most companies now circulate compilations of platitudes, euphemisms, and slogans (the likes of: "to better understand our clients' needs") that have been formalized into supposedly inspirational mission statements. No one ever reads these, which is the running joke of the 1996 movie *Jerry Maguire*, in which Tom Cruise plays a sports agent who keeps apologizing to colleagues for having suggested that quality might be more important than quantity: "It was just a mission statement!" See: CORPORATION, PPCV

 CORPORATION A legally sanctioned entity, most often used to conduct business, which – though immortal, unless "dissolved" – has its own status and rights like a natural person. Critics argue that granting personhood to an organization with no personal liability creates a Frankenstein monster: a legal entity without any moral or legal responsibility to encourage restraint, yet with the ability and resources to exploit natural resources, co-opt public policy, and wreak havoc on communities. Legal scholar Joel Bakan has described the modern *corporation* as a "psychopath." See: CORPORATE VALUES

CORVÉE *Corvée* is unpaid labor that in medieval and early modern Europe was imposed upon serfs and villeins, by aristocrats and nobles, in lieu of taxation. The term has its origins in the late Roman Empire, during which time a landlord could demand *opera corrogata* ("requisitioned work") of his tenants. Technically, corvée isn't slave labor: though unfree, such labor is usually intermittent; and other than in the dispensation of his or her labor, the worker is free. I use the present tense because corvée labor still exists as such in Myanmar and Bhutan, and also in the form of military conscription, prison labor, and (arguably) jury duty elsewhere. See: REPARTIMIENTO, WAGE SLAVERY

 COWORKING When *freelancers* (sorry, *free agents*), nomadic Internet entrepreneurs, and work-at-home professionals share an office space, it's known as *coworking*. Not to be confused with a "business incubator" space, a

coworking space is as much about socializing and community as it is about, you know, getting work done. But what the hell – it's got to be better than *hot desking*, or working in a *cube farm*. See: CUBE FARM, HOT DESKING

CREDENTIALISM Whereas most blue-collar occupations have traditionally used an apprentice system for purposes of hiring and promoting workers, employers of white-collar workers often require of prospective employees not practical experience but a diploma, academic degree, or professional license. Critics of *credentialism* claim that employers who require credentials may be using those requirements as a social class screen, i.e., discriminating against lower-class applicants. Other victims of punitive credentialism include surgeons and engineers from underdeveloped countries who wind up driving a taxicab when they emigrate. See: COLLAR (BLUE OR WHITE), DISCRIMINATION (EMPLOYMENT)

CROP DUSTING Surreptitiously releasing a silent fart (*assassination, church fart, S.B.D., scooter, silent but violent, toxic streamer*) while walking through a *cube farm*. Note that releasing a silent fart while sitting is called *laying an egg* or a *one-cheek sneak*. See: CUBE FARM

CUBE FARM A pejorative workplace slang term – dating to the dotcom era – meaning "a featureless, modern office filled with rows of identical cubicles." Also known as a *sea of cubicles*, cube farms have been satirized in sci-fi movies like *Tron* and *The Matrix*; in *Generation X*, Douglas Coupland dubbed them *veal-fattening pens*. See: CUBICLE (OFFICE), PRAIRIE DOGGING

CUBICLE (OFFICE) A flexible, semi-enclosed workspace first sold by Herman Miller in 1964-77 under the moniker "Action Office." Designed by Robert Probst, who consulted with mathematicians, behavioral psychologists, and anthropologists, the *cubicle* was designed to promote personal initiative and employee interaction. This was utopian, space-age stuff: in fact, the first appearance of an Action Office product was in Stanley Kubrick's *2001: A Space Odyssey*. However, cubicles have since come to be widely regarded as emblems of uniformity and blandness; Probst reportedly later regretted his contribution to what he called "monolithic insanity." See: CUBE FARM

DATSU-SARA This Japanese neologism (from *datsu*, "remove, take off," and *sara*, an abbreviation of the word for salary man) refers to the act of quitting a boring, unfulfilling office job in order to be one's own boss, by doing something entrepreneurial. Until the 1990s, guaranteed lifetime employment was the norm in Japan; since then, however, the *datsu-sara* trend has been on the rise. See: DOWN-SHIFTER

 DEVIL Archaic slang verb meaning "perform routine work for another." Mostly encountered in the form of a noun, as in *printer's devil*, an apprentice in a printing establishment who mixed tubs of ink, fetched type, and did other grunt work. (Benjamin Franklin disliked being a printer's devil so much that he ran away from Boston to Philadelphia at 17, where a few years later set up his own printing house.) Why "devil"? It's a mystery, though some suggest that it's because printing ink stained the apprentices' skin as dark as the devil's supposedly is. See: WAYZGOOSE

DICKENSIAN Charles Dickens's name has become an eponym, thanks to his unforgettable portrayal of the horrid work and living conditions of Victorian-era England's poor. However, Dickens distrusted revolutionary movements, labor strikes, and other forms of class conflict; he hoped instead to ameliorate the failures of his society via charity and reform. In an 1854 essay about a millworkers' strike, Dickens expressed his view "that into the relations between employers and employed, as into all the relations in this life, there must enter something of feeling and sentiment"; in *Hard Times*, written that same year, he portrays the mill owner Mr. Bounderby and the utilitarian educator Mr. Gradgrind as misguided, not wicked. See: GUOLAOSI

DILBERT Neologism trackers tell us that to *dilbert* someone is to make him cynical about work. For example, in a cynical 1995 *Wall Street Journal* article, Adams defined "the Dilbert principle" as the tendency of companies to systematically promote their least competent employees to management. But Tom Vanderbilt has pointed out, in a *Baffler* essay, that the titular character of Scott Adams' popular comic strip isn't cynical about corporate values; instead, what frustrates him is the inefficient realization of those values. Paraphrasing T.W. Adorno's analysis of Thorstein Veblen, we might say of Adams that his "critique of 'institutions' is uncompromising, but he seems to be so fascinated by [workplace efficiency] that it... endangers the humanity which [efficiency] is supposed to serve." See: EFFICIENCY, JOB SATISFACTION

DINKUM (FAIR) First recorded in the 1890s, scholars claim that this Australian slang phrase (which now means "speaking the truth," or "authentic," and which, by the way, is mostly used by Australians in jest) originated with a now-extinct dialect word from the East Midlands in England, where *dinkum* meant "hard work," or "fair share of work." Another fun British term that has survived only in Australia is *bludger*, meaning "slacker," which is to say "someone who doesn't do her dinkum." See: WALLABY (ON THE)

DISCRIMINATION (EMPLOYMENT) Discrimination in hiring, promotion, job assignment, termination, and compensation on the basis of, e.g., race, ethnicity, sex, age, disability, or sexual orientation. At the risk of seeming to make light of this problem, it's amusing to note that the great Slick Rick raps about an inverse form of *employment discrimination* in his un-PC 1994 song, "Get a Job": "And you can't be gentle, or they get all sentimental/ 'I don't work for white people,' 'Well, work for Orientals!'" See: DISCRIMINATION (WAGE), GLASS CEILING

DISCRIMINATION (WAGE) Two laws protect workers against *wage discrimination*: the Equal Pay Act of 1963, which prohibits unequal pay for equal or substantially equal work performed by men and women; and Title VII of the Civil Rights Act of 1964, which prohibits wage discrimination (even when the jobs are not identical) on the basis of race, color, sex, religion, or national origin. However, studies show that the more an occupation is dominated by women or people of color, the less it pays; and although the men/women wage gap in the US has narrowed, since 1973 approximately 60 percent of that change is due to the fall in men's real earnings. See: DISCRIMINATION (EMPLOYMENT)

 DIY The *DIY* movement is descended from the postwar bourgeois craze for hands-on home improvement, car repair, and other hobbies; in the 1960s, it was co-opted by the authenticity-mongering counterculture – and popularized by Stewart Brand's *The Whole Earth Catalog*. In the '70s, doing it yourself became a mainstream fad again, only to be co-opted again in the '80s by hardcore punks. Mark Frauenfelder, editor of the magazine *MAKE*, boils the appeal of DIY down to: "(1) a deeper connection to the things that keep us alive and well, (2) an appreciation for the things you have and the systems that make it possible, (3) an opportunity to use your hands and your brain, (4) a connection to other people, and (5) a path to freedom." It is the last point that explains why countercultural types keep rediscovering DIY, and also why the term belongs in this *Glossary*. See: AUTONOMISM

DOG (FUCKING THE) One or two reviews of *The Idler's Glossary*, this author's compendium of glosses on idleness-related terms, neologisms, and euphemisms, lamented the omission of the British-Canadian slang term *fucking the dog*, which means "procrastinating on the job." Though *The Idler's Glossary* does include an entry on the phrase *screwing the pooch*, the author apologizes for the omission. See: *The Idler's Glossary*

 DOG (SEEING A MAN ABOUT A) In *Flying Scud*, an 1866 horse-racing drama by the Irish actor-playwright Dion Boucicault, which ran for two hundred nights in London, a character explains his imminent departure from a sticky situation with a phony excuse: "I've got to see a man about a dog," a euphemism meaning that he needs to place a bet on a dog. The phrase caught on among those inclined to see absenteeism as no big deal; at the University of Toronto, one hears, the phrase also means "I need to pee." See: ABSENTEEISM

DONE-DONE Today's younger workers, who came of age during an era of grade inflation, reportedly share a tendency to describe a project as "done" when it's not. That explains this recent workplace coinage, which means "truly, properly completed." See: FUNEMPLOYED, SLACKOISIE

DOWN-NESTING In his novel *Generation X*, Douglas Coupland uses this original coinage to describe the tendency of his generation's parents to move to smaller, guest-room-free houses after their children have grown up – i.e., so as to avoid sheltering their children, whose life prospects are less rosy than their own were at that same age. See: MCJOB

DOWNSHIFTER From the mid-1980s through the mid-1990s, journalists and academics wrote endlessly about "downshifting" professionals – who'd quit demanding careers in order to practice "voluntary simplicity." Though we were supposed to believe that a societal paradigm shift was underway, in retrospect it's apparent that this was just a sanctimonious moment in the Baby Boomers' collective midlife crisis. See: DATSU-SARA

DOWNSIZING Perhaps the most frequently used administrative euphemism meaning the "termination of employment for an employee or group of employees due to business reasons." Also known as: *decruitment, delayering, early retirement, force shaping, headcount adjustment, offshoring* (or *bestshoring*), *rightsizing* or *smartsizing, operational simplification, personnel realignment, rationalizing the workforce, recussion, reduction in force* (RIF), *skill mix adjustment, workforce optimization,* and *workforce reduction* (WFR). All I can add to this list is: WTF? See: ADMIN, LAYOFF

 DOWNTIME By the 1980s, this midcentury term, which originally meant "time when a machine is out of action or unavailable for use," had been adopted by managers describing the unavailability of "human capital," i.e., workers. Which suggests that human beings who aren't working are best compared to machines being serviced or robots being recharged. Worse, many of us now blithely use *downtime* to describe our own weekends, vacations, and other moments of leisure. See: BANDWIDTH, ROBOT

DUNG In 18th-c. British workmen's slang, a *dung* is a worker (often a journeyman) who accepts wages below the standard customary in society at that time. Today, perhaps we might apply the term to

affluent young college grads whose willingness to work cheaply at, say, New York media jobs, keeps wages low. See: BLACKLEG, FLINT

EFFICIENCY A quantitative concept, not to be confused with the qualitative term *effectiveness*, describing the extent to which time and/or effort produces a specific outcome for an intended task or purpose with a minimum amount of waste and/or expense. Efficiency is well and good in its place – one thinks of energy and thermal conservation, data storage, lift-to-drag ratio – but it's too often subject to mission creep. During the Progressive Era, for example, the Efficiency Movement in the US, Britain and other industrial nations proposed to eliminate waste and implement best practices not merely in the economic, but the social sphere. See: ASSEMBLY LINE, TAYLORISM, THERBLIG

EMPIRE BUILDING Any effort on the part of a white-collar worker or coterie of workers to make it more difficult for their employer to lay them off by (a) gaining control over key projects and initiatives, and (b) hoarding credit and prestige, no matter how deleterious the effect of doing so may be to the company and other workers. See: CAREERISM, OFFICE POLITICS

EMPLOYEE Legally speaking: "a person in the service of another under any contract of hire, express or implied, oral or written, where the employer has the right to control and direct the employee in the material details of how the work is to be performed." From a political-philosophical perspective: a pitiable wage slave. See: WAGE SLAVERY

EMPLOYEE ENGAGEMENT The decline in job security and benefits since the 1980s has required businesses to find new means to keep employees motivated not only to do their job, but also to put forth extra effort. Hence the current fad for *employee engagement* programs, which promote such novel concepts as listening to workers, expanding workers' responsibilities, and coaching and mentoring. Usually a stopgap measure, they're regarded as a distraction and waste of time by most employees – who are more interested in job security, committed top management, and corporate integrity. See: JOB ENLARGEMENT, WORKPLACE DEMOCRACY

EMPLOYEE OF THE MONTH A business award given to dutiful employees in lieu of more tangible rewards. The award is widely regarded as an empty gesture, or as an honor one is embarrassed to receive... which explains

why this phrase has been used as the title of satirical movies and record albums, and why the practice has been mocked in episodes of nearly every sitcom in the history of American television. See: BROWN-NOSE, CAN-DO

EYESERVICE Working only when the boss is watching, an ancient practice noted in Colossians 3:22. "Servants, obey in all things your masters according to the flesh; not with eyeservice, as men-pleasers; but in singleness of heart, fearing God." See: SLOWDOWN, SURVEILLANCE (WORKPLACE)

FACTOTUM A cod Latin term meaning "man of all work," or "general servant." Charles Bukowski's 1975 novel of that title follows the exploits of a would-be author who takes on one menial job after another, in 1940s Los Angeles. The first employment ad to which he responds is couched in the vaguest terms: "Need ambitious young man with an eye to the future. Exper. not necessary." See: GIG, LABOR (UNSKILLED)

FIRED To be *terminated, given the boot, let go, canned, cashiered, axed, shown the door, bounced out.* In corporate jargon: *early retirement, forced resignation, assignment ended,*

position eliminated, released from the talent pool, made available to industry, one-person layoff, contract not renewed, relieved of duties. Also: to go *off the box*, a phrase derived from Kellogg's decision to remove disgraced Olympic swimmer Michael Phelps' photo from Corn Flakes boxes. See: DOWNSIZING, SACK (GETTING THE)

FLEXECUTIVE A mid-1990s coinage meaning "an executive whose hours and place of work are flexible." Though telecommuting to Microsoft from a virtual office in Brooklyn or Miami was supposed to be the cat's pajamas, in a *Baffler* article Tom Vanderbilt dismissed all the hype around the *flexecutive* fad as a "Panglossian declaration of Third Wave theorists." For one thing, telecommuters sometimes work longer hours. That's why a 2004 study of male and female IT professionals found that although the majority of them wanted more flexibility in their working practices, they didn't think their senior managers made good work-life-balance role models. See: COMMUTING, OFFICING

FLEXIBILIZATION This euphemistic bit of corporate jargon (short for: "flexible specialization") refers to corporations' practice of seeking employment relations that permit them easily to increase or diminish their workforce, and reassign and redeploy workers. If in the past century or so the typical corporate strategy of the industrial society was uniform mass production with Taylor-esque structures and stable employment, the typical corporate strategy of the 21st century looks likely to be *flexibilization*. Which suggests that the 21st-century workforce will be characterized by an elite few who enjoy unlimited full employment, and an ever-growing group of short-term, limited- and/or part-time workers who face severe employment risks. See: KUDOKA

FLEXTIME Originally, *flextime* (derived from *Gleitzeit*, a German neologism) meant "a variable work schedule under which employees are only expected to be at work during a certain 4- or 5-hour period of the day, as long the necessary work gets done." However under a 2004 flextime proposal from the George W. Bush administration employers would not be required to pay non-exempt employees overtime for working, say, 70 hours one week so long as they worked 10 hours or less the following week. (What was that sound? Yep, it was the other shoe dropping.) Taking a *flex day* is known, at least in Australia, as *flexing*. See: PERKS

FLIGHT RISK Ribald workplace descriptor for an employee suspected of planning to leave the company soon. It seems important, at this juncture in the *Glossary*, to remark upon how often the workplace is implicitly or explicitly compared to a prison or plantation. See: ASSEMBLY LINE, CORVÉE

 FLINT Archaic workmen's slang meaning "worker who is paid fair wages by prevailing standards." To "flint it out" was to insist on full wages. It is ironic, then, that the city of Flint, Michigan, birthplace of General Motors (and the Flint Sit-Down Strike of 1936-37 that played a vital role in the formation of the United Auto Workers), has today become a sad symbol of the decline of the labor movement's efficacy. See: DUNG

FORDISM The term gives credit to Henry Ford for what he did to make American life revolve around production and consumption, thus producing sustained economic growth and widespread material advancement. But *Fordism* is also a cultural phenomenon: i.e., Marxist critics claim that, in order for Ford's mechanized assembly line production to function properly, workers were indoctrinated to internalize the disciplined regularity of the machines they tended. Aldous Huxley's 1932 science fiction novel *Brave New World* pushes this conceit further: in it, the World State is built on the principles of mass production and the consumption of disposable consumer goods... and Fordism has become an ascetic religion. See: DOWNTIME, TAYLORISM

FOSSICK How to describe the activity of the desperate new breed of "entrepreneurial journalists" who spend their days and nights rapidly extruding "articles" about community news, pets, and Justin Bieber – that is, lame content designed to generate ad revenue – for a penny-per-pageview? This bit of Australian-ese (actually a bastardized piece of English dialect), which means "work an abandoned mining claim, wash old dirt in search of gold," fits the bill nicely. See: WORK (DRUDGE)

 FREE AGENT In the 1996 movie *Jerry Maguire*, Cuba Gooding Jr. plays a wide receiver who becomes a free agent rather than accept a less-than-amazing contract; in the end, he is rewarded for his resolve and daring. In a *Fast Company* cover story a few months later, motivational writer Daniel H. Pink dubbed self-employed workers, independent contractors, and temps "free agents," thus explicitly likening them to pro athletes who can ratchet up their salaries by sparking bidding wars among would-be employers. Job security, enthused Pink, was nothing to be mourned. See: FREELANCER, GIGONOMICS, HIRELING

FREELANCER A *freelancer* is a self-employed person (or "open-collar worker") who pursues a profession without a long-term commitment to any particular employer. The term has morphed from a noun (Sir Walter Scott coined the term "free lance," or roving knight, in *Ivanhoe*) into an adjective (e.g., "a freelance journalist"), then into a verb (e.g., "a journalist who freelances"), then into an adverb (e.g., "she worked freelance"), and then back into a noun: "freelancer." Freedom is important to freelancers; however, let's not romanticize them. *Ivanhoe*'s Maurice De Bracy, leader of the Free Lances, is a mercenary villain, described as a man "whose profession freed him from all scruples"; also, as the 2010 *Star Wars*-related meme reminds us: "Boba Fett was a freelancer." See: FREE AGENT

FREETER A pejorative or pitying Japanese neologism dating to the 1980s, the term *freeter* is derived from the English loanword "freelance" and the German-Japanese term *arubaito* ("part-time job").

It's used to refer to anyone, other than homemakers and students, who lacks full-time employment or is unemployed. See: FREELANCER

FRIDAY (CASUAL) In his 1997 history, *The Conquest of Cool*, Thomas Frank argues persuasively that the counterculture of the 1960s-'70s wasn't co-opted but instead *invented* by ad-men and marketers, who perceived in the Boomer-led cultural revolution "a comrade in their own struggles to revitalize American business and the consumer order generally." It turns out that the same thing goes for the origins of Casual Friday, an institution which was the result of a campaign in the late 1970s by clothing manufacturers seeking to unload blue jeans and Hawaiian shirts. See: WORKWEEK

FUNEMPLOYED "For the 'funemployed,' unemployment is welcome," read a *Los Angeles Times* headline in June 2009. At a time when millions of Americans struggled to find work as they faced foreclosures and bankruptcy, the neologism *funemployment* appeared seemingly overnight in the Twitter feeds of happily jobless men and women in their 20s and 30s. For a generation whose sky-high self-esteem won't permit them to take jobs they deem unworthy of their talents, the recession had removed the stigma of unemployment

– and, perhaps, of downward mobility, too. See: SLACKOISIE

GETI JINGJI Until the late 1970s, the powers that be in China refused to admit even the possibility, much less the existence of a private sector: i.e., businesses and other enterprises run by private individuals or groups, and not controlled by the state. Today, Chinese newspapers are full of stories about the *geti jingji*, the emerging class of entrepreneurial business owners and self-employed workers. See: FREE AGENT

GHERAO Derived from a Bengali term meaning "encirclement," *gherao* is a South Asian mode of protest (dating to the late 1960s) in which workers prevent employers from leaving their place of work until their demands are met. Ironically, employers in some developing countries, who've physically prevented workers from leaving a workplace, first invented this practice – known as a *lock-in*. See: BANDH, BOSSNAPPING, LOCKOUT

GIG A temporary piece of work, the advantages of which are: ease of being hired (no selection process, as long as one is qualified), flexible hours, and sometimes a pay rate that is higher than the customary wages in a comparable permanent position. Once, the term for this sort of employment was *job*; today, it's more and more likely that one's job (formerly: profession or occupation) is nothing but a *gig*. See: GIGONOMICS, JOB

GIGONOMICS A neologism, introduced in January 2009 by Tina Brown, suggesting that we've entered an era in which everyone has a *gig* instead of a *job*. Many of us were already living paycheck to paycheck, of course; Brown was moved to coin this term when she discovered that even college-educated Americans who earn more than $75,000 a year are now working either freelance or two jobs. *Newsweek* enthused, later that same month: "A new generation of workers has 24/7 connectivity, lacks corporate loyalty, and thinks like mavericks." See: FREE AGENT, GIG

GLASS CEILING The limited advancement of a qualified individual (a woman, when the phrase was coined in the 1980s; today, the phrase is widely applicable) within the hierarchy of an organization because of discrimination, including different pay for comparable work, harassment, and lack of family-friendly workplace policies. Related terms: *bamboo ceiling* (for Asian-Americans), *brass ceiling* (in the military), *concrete ceiling* (for minority women), *gray ceiling* (for the Boomers' immediate juniors), *stained-glass ceiling* (in religious organizations), *glass cliff* (for women who've broken through the glass ceiling only to be saddled with an extra-high risk of failure), and *glass closet* (for openly gay men and women). See: DISCRIMINATION (EMPLOYMENT)

GRAFT Archaic term that once meant "hard, unrelenting, persistent work." Derived from a British dialect word meaning "to dig," which comes from the Anglo-Saxon verb *grafan*, in its noun form *graft* came to mean "ditch," i.e., the result of such work. In America, graft means "dishonesty, bribery" – perhaps, some lexicographers suggest, because the influence-peddling grafter gets his shovel in and digs away. See: PROFESSION (ADAM'S), WORK (DRUDGE)

GRAVY TRAIN In the 1920s, when "gravy" was slang for "easy money," railroad workers coined this phrase to refer to a cushy job; even cushier was a *gravy train* with biscuit wheels on it. But at least since Pink Floyd's 1975 album *Wish You Were Here*, the phrase has also connoted everything that's wrong with the Establishment. On that album, the lyrics of the song "Have a Cigar" are written in the voice of a cynical music executive co-opting youth, rebelliousness, artistry: "And did we tell you the name of the game, boy? We call it Riding the Gravy Train." See: AMBITION

 GREYBEARDING The loss of knowledge caused by the ageing and retirement of those workers who know the logic and rationale of the way things are done. Younger workers, even if better educated and more highly credentialed, lack such knowledge. See: BRIGHT-SIZING, RETIREMENT (ACCIDENTAL)

GRIND Mid-19th-c. slang meaning "hard, continuous, wearing work," as in the slang phrase *daily grind* (i.e., employment). From the 1910s through the '50s, a hard worker might be described as a *grind*; since then, however, the term has only been used to describe hard-working undergrads and hockey players. Recently, the term slipped back into the world of work via video gaming, where players will "grind" (engage in repetitive and/or non-entertaining gameplay) in order to gain access to other features. As work becomes more virtual, video games become more like work! See: GRIND (RISE AND), PLAYBOR

GRIND (RISE AND) A phrase employed every morning by umpteen thousands of Twitter users; it's meant to broadcast the fact that they're out of bed and getting their day started. See: GRIND, GTFBTW

GRINDING HOUSE A 19th-c. slang term meaning "place of business or work." It's fascinating to learn that in the 17th and 18th centuries, *grinding house* was slang for "house of correction, where one works as part of one's punishment." Once again, we find wage slavery implicitly or explicitly compared to prison life – very telling, isn't it? See: ASSEMBLY LINE, STOPPO

GTFBTW Online slang meaning, "Get the fuck back to work." See: SLACKOISIE

GUOLAOSI Mandarin neologism meaning "over-work death" – a fate that befalls an estimated 600,000 Chinese factory workers a year, one reads in *China Daily*. Manufacturing goods for the western world for eighteen hours a day in Dickensian conditions, the fatigued workers fall off their stools, bleeding from ears, nose, and anus, and die. See: BREAK

HANG FIRE "In the sweet old country where I come from/ Nobody ever works/ Yeah nothing gets done/ We hang fire...." This late 18th-c. British slang phrase once referred to guns that were slow in communicating the fire through the vent to the charge. By the time the Rolling Stones put *hang fire* into the title of one of their few overtly political songs, about England's economic malaise, the term had come to connote "doing nothing, because of structural unemployment." See: UNEMPLOYMENT

HAWTHORNE EFFECT From 1924-1932 researchers at the Hawthorne Works outside Chicago sought to determine whether factory workers were more productive in higher or lower levels of illumination; productivity improved during the study, then slumped once it was over. It has been suggested that the productivity gain was due to the motivational effect of the interest being shown in the workers – i.e., no matter what changes the researchers made, the result would have been an increase in productivity. Hm. Here's what the study illuminated: the alienated character of factory work. See: ALIENATION, JOB SATISFACTION

HEADCOUNT REDUCTIONS One of many euphemistic phrases meaning "termination of employment due to business reasons." Here's a November 2008 example of the phrase in use: "Nokia Siemens Networks has completed the preliminary planning process to identify the proposed remaining headcount reductions necessary to reach its previously announced synergy-related headcount adjustment goal." Ugh. See: DOWNSIZING

HIRELING America's transition, in the first half of the 19th century, from a nation of independent small producers to wage labor, deeply troubled those republicans who believed that a free government and a populace that was cowed and mercenary were incompatible. "No refuge could save the hireling and the slave/ From the terror of flight, or the gloom of the grave": this couplet from Francis Scott Key's "The Star-Spangled Banner" castigates the British army, which during the War of 1812 used freed slaves and hireling soldiers. Webster's 1829 dictionary of American English gives "prostitute" as a synonym for hireling; as an adjective, *hireling* meant both venal and mercenary. Back then, only a jeremiad would have a title like Daniel H. Pink's 1990s manifesto: *Free Agent Nation.* See: FREE AGENT, FREELANCER, WAGE LABOR

 HOLIDAY (BLIND MAN'S) Until the invention of whale spermaceti candles in the mid-18th century, the workday was tied to the sun; when you could no longer see your work, labor stopped. This archaic term refers to that time

of day when it's too dark to see, but not yet dark enough to light lanterns – so a break from work is taken. Today, it's never too dark to work. With every advance in artificial illumination since the 18th century, we've trained ourselves to sleep and dream less while working more. See: BREAK

HOLIDAY (BUSMAN'S) In 19th-c. London, some bus drivers rode their own horse-drawn buses on their days off, just to make sure that other drivers weren't mistreating the animals. That's cute, but let's face it: spending your free time doing the same thing you do during working hours is lame. In the 1940s, T.W. Adorno claimed that the hectic pace of our so-called leisure activities is "the reflex-action to a production rhythm imposed heteronymously on the subject, compulsively maintained even in the weary pauses." True: mechanized workers don't easily turn back into humans. See: DOWNTIME, FORDISM

HORSE When a workman charges for more in his week's work than he has really done, it's known (in archaic slang) as *horse*. See: NOSEBAG (PUT ON THE)

HORSE (DEAD) A mid-17th-c. slang term referring to "work that has already been paid for but has yet to be done." If you've accepted an advance on your wages (i.e., in sailors' slang, a *compo*), and must now pay it off, you're riding a *dead horse*. See: HORSE

HOT DESKING When more than one sailor is assigned to a "rack" (bunk) on a cramped sailing ship or submarine, it's called *hot racking* – because your bunk is still hot when you lie down. Gross! In the late 1980s, when businesses whose employees weren't always in the office began assigning several workers to a single desk, a similar phrase caught on to describe this practice. Which also seems gross. See: COWORKING

HOUR-GLASS CEILING A time-based impediment to career advancement, faced mostly by working mothers – who, on average, spend more time caring for children than working fathers do. See: GLASS CEILING, TIME BIND

HUMAN CAPITAL The Chicago School economist Gary Becker's 1964 treatise of that title likened investment in worker education and training to investment in the means of production; additional investment in your workers' competence and well-being, according to this influential theory, yields a higher rate of return. *Human capital*, a concept dating back to Adam Smith, can also be said to comprise such inalienable traits as skill, creativity, enterprise, courage, even wisdom and empathy. When those individuals with the most valuable competences and traits leave a city or country, it's known as "brain drain" or "human capital flight." See: HUMAN RESOURCES

HUMAN RELATIONS A school of thought, which emerged in the 1930s, arguing that social interaction patterns, and not merely economic rewards or skill specialization, are critical in determining work productivity. For the first time, organizations were viewed by efficiency experts not as mechanical contraptions but human cooperative systems. Enter such half-baked concepts as "group dynamics" and "people skills." See: ALIENATION

HUMAN RESOURCES HR professionals would have us believe that *Human Resources* as we know it – i.e., the administrative and strategic management of an organization's personnel – began in reaction to the dehumanizing efficiency focus of Taylorism. Yet in a 1915 article in *The Times* (London), we find the earliest recorded use of the term: "Side by side with the committees that have been set up to deal with the production of material there should be an organization to take stock of the human resources still at the disposal of the nation." Which sounds awfully efficient. See: ADMIN, PLANTATION

 HUMP DAY Wage slaves' slang term for Wednesday – i.e., that point in the workweek to which you have struggled uphill since Monday morning, and from which you will presumably coast downhill through Friday afternoon. See: WORKWEEK

HURRY SICKNESS It's dispiriting to discover that the contemporary malaise known as "hurry sickness," victims of which feel chronically short of time, was first identified in the 1950s. Half-a-century and a computer revolution later, and we're still so busy? See: LEISURE SICKNESS

INCENTIVIZE Corporate jargon (coined in 1968) for "motivate," i.e., by some combination of carrot and stick. Winston Churchill reputedly once said, "Naval tradition? Monstrous. Nothing but rum, sodomy, and the lash." Now, *that's* what I call incentivizing. See: PRIGUISTICS

INCOME For individuals and households, the sum of all wages and other forms of earnings received in a given period of time. The emphasis in that phrase should be on "other forms of earnings," since the true difference between the rich and the poor has nothing to do with intelligence, natural gifts, or effort; instead, it has much to do with 'unearned revenue,' including interest and dividends from investments, rent, and so forth. In Jane Austen novels – haven't you ever noticed? – the term *income* is rarely, if ever used in connection with a character's wages or salary. See: CITIZEN'S DIVIDEND

INCOME (BASIC) A proposed system whereby the government would guarantee that each citizen has enough income to meet her basic needs. The French economist and philosopher André Gorz has argued, in his 1989 anti-wage-slavery treatise, *Critique of Economic Reason*, that because it is no longer necessary to work as hard as it once was to produce the necessities of life, a basic income ought to be guaranteed so that workers would be free to produce less, while spending more time enjoying "air, water, space, silence, beauty, time, and human contact." See: CITIZEN'S DIVIDEND

 INEMURI The workplace power nap, Japanese-style. The term, which means "sleeping while present," refers to an accepted custom: dozing while seated in an upright position

at one's desk. Doing *inemuri* demonstrates that you've been working late; doing it while sitting up demonstrates that you are still socially engaged. See: SHIFT (GRAVEYARD, LOBSTER)

INSPECTOR OF PAVEMENTS This 19th-c. slang phrase refers, snarkily, to a man of out of work. See: PATTIN' LEATHER

INTERNSHIP "Interns Built the Pyramids!" blared the spine of *The Baffler* #9 (1997). To this succinct criticism of the farce we call *internship*, nothing more need be added. See: STRIKE (SERVILITY)

JACK OF ALL TRADES Well before Fordism, workers resistant to specialization were subjected to concerted propaganda efforts. For example: from the early 17th century until the heyday of industrialization, a *jack* (informal British term for "trade laborer") capable of doing many tasks well was highly esteemed. But then, to the jaunty phrase "jack of all trades" was appended the unflattering postscript "and master of none." Don't believe the hype. In Terry Gilliam's dystopian 1985 movie, *Brazil*, Robert De Niro plays a heroic jack of all trades in a convoluted and inefficient social order overseen by over-specialized bureaucrats: he's a masterless man. See: ALIENATION, ASSEMBLY LINE

JOB According to the *OED*, the word *job* is earliest attested in the 1557 phrase "Doinge certen Iobbes of woorke." And in the 18th and 19th centuries, the term was thieves' cant meaning "a planned-out burglary or robbery" (from which we get the shady phrase *job lot*). In other words, a job used to be a small, discrete piece of work; today, it's a paid position of regular employment, labor performed day in and day out, from 9 a.m. to 5 p.m., sometimes for one's entire adult life. The increased duration of jobs has taken its toll, as is articulated by "Wizard" (Peter Boyle) in *Taxi Driver*: "A man takes a job, you know? And that job – I mean, like that – that becomes what he is. [...] You got no choice, anyway. I mean, we're all fucked." PS: Note that *gig* now means what *job* originally meant. See: GIG

JOB (FIXING THE) Wobbly slang referring to quickie strikes, passive resistance, deliberate bungling and other methods employed by workers seeking better conditions or pay. Patti Smith's 1974 song "Piss Factory" alludes to this sort of thing: "Floor boss slides up to me and he says/

'Hey sister, you just movin' too fast,/ You screwin' up the quota,/ You doin' your piecework too fast,/ Now you get off your mustang sally.'" The King Missile song "Take Stuff from Work," though, is merely about slacking off: "It's your duty as an oppressed worker to steal from your exploiters./ It's gonna be an outstanding day./ Take stuff from work./ And goof off on company time." See: WOBBLIES, SLOWDOWN

JOB CLINGING A 2010 analysis by the Employee Benefit Research Institute shows workers' median length of time on the job rose markedly during the recent recession. Aging Baby Boomers, in particular, have clung to their existing positions; among men aged 60 to 64 still working full time, 56.8% had held their current job for 10 years or more, up from 48.1% four years earlier. That's bad news for younger workers, who face a so-called "gray ceiling" formed by unmoving Boomers. See: GLASS CEILING

JOB EMBEDDEDNESS The term refers to the degree to which employees are "enmeshed" in their jobs, i.e., how well their jobs utilize their skills, how likely it is that they will achieve their life goals within the organization, how effective their workgroup is, and so forth. A 2009 study found that low levels of *job embeddedness* can be highly contagious. See: JOB ENLARGEMENT

JOB ENLARGEMENT In order to address the symptoms (though not the causes) of worker alienation and demotivation, around mid-century employees in repetitive jobs began to be allocated tasks involving greater variety, complexity, and responsibility. This contradicted the principles of specialization and the division of labor, but the argument was that the efficiency gained by these methods was offset by inefficiencies traceable to workers' unhappiness. Results have shown that, over time, even an enlarged job role can become boring; but continuing to enlarge a worker's job (known as "job creep") can result in a massive workload. See: BOREOUT, JOB ENRICHMENT

JOB ENRICHMENT In the 1960s, efficiency experts designed jobs and organizational structures to replace the skill-fragmenting industrial bureaucracies of the post-WWII era. As opposed to *job enlargement*, which attempts to motivate workers by increasing the number of tasks they perform, *job enrichment* attempts to motivate by giving workers meaningful tasks, a range of challenges, and plenty of feedback. See: JOB ENLARGEMENT

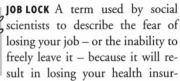 **JOB LOCK** A term used by social scientists to describe the fear of losing your job – or the inability to freely leave it – because it will result in losing your health insurance. Since most Americans receive health insurance through their employers, and because employer-provided health insurance is nonportable, the phrase *job lock* is tautological: to have a job is to be locked into it. See: BENEFITS (EMPLOYEE), JOB CLINGING

JOB PRECARIOUSNESS "Precariousness is good," a 1970s autonomist motto boldly proclaims. "Job precariousness is a form of autonomy from steady regular work, lasting an entire life," explains the Italian autonomist theorist Franco Berardi (Bifo). "In the 1970s many people used to work for a few months, then to go away for a journey, then back to work for a while. This was possible in times of almost full employment and in times of egalitarian culture." But not, alas, any longer. See: AUTONOMISM, ROUSTABOUT

JOB SATISFACTION Management style, workplace culture, plus employee empowerment are key factors contributing to an elusive existential condition: *job satisfaction*. Beginning in the 1930s, job-satisfaction researchers hypothesized that *people work for purposes other than pay*. What could such other purposes possibly be? It wasn't until 1943 that the psychologist Abraham Maslow announced that once we've satisfied our physiological and safety needs, humans seek love and belonging, esteem, and self-actualization. Can work provide these? Seems unlikely: "I was looking for a job, and then I found a job," sings Morrissey in the Smiths' song whose title is taken from the next line: "And heaven knows I'm miserable now." See: BURNOUT, TAYLORISM

JOB SECURITY The probability that an individual will keep his or her job. Generally speaking, *job security* is high in times of economic expansion and lower in times of a recession; it is a much-lamented phenomenon, these days. Though not, of course, by idlers. See: JOB PRECARIOUSNESS

KAIZEN From the Japanese *kai* ("change") and *zen* ("good"), this successful implementation of *continuous improvement process* was popularized by Masaaki "the Lean Guru" Imai's 1986 book of that title. The idea of *kaizen* is that new ideas come from the workers (i.e., they're not based on R&D, or from consultants) and that changes are limited to small, incremental improvements. However, critics claim that companies use *kaizen* as a way to avoid making changes. See: CIP

KEEPING UP WITH THE JONESES This 19th-c. phrase, which means "comparing one's accumulation of material goods to one's neighbors or social equals," was popularized by a comic strip of that title which first appeared in 1913. The Joneses never appeared in the strip – the point being, perhaps, that "the Joneses" are an ever-receding ideal. See: AMBITION

 KNOCK OFF WORK The phrase, which means "quit work for the day," originated in the days of ships propelled by oarsmen. To keep the oarsmen rowing in unison, a man with the gift of perfect rhythm would beat time on a block of wood; when it was time to rest or change shifts, he'd give a special knock. The meme began to go viral circa 1902. See: WAGE SLAVERY

KUDOKA A Japanese term describing the post-industrial trend, described by MIT economist David Autor as "job polarization," in which society loses its moderately skilled workforce: e.g., bank tellers, cashiers, typists, appliance repairmen, and other occupations that only require a high-school degree. Which is not to suggest that all those high-school graduates are working at highly skilled jobs, instead. See: FLEXIBILIZATION, OUTSOURCING

KURZARBEIT In several European countries facing economic recessions, the government has recently helped cover employees' lost wages in exchange for businesses' agreement to reduce working hours for everyone – i.e., instead of laying people off. Proponents of *Kurzarbeit* (German for "short-work") argue that it keeps people in jobs, thus preventing their skills from atrophying. See: FLEXTIME, LAYOFF

LABOR "One of the processes by which A acquires property for B." So notes Ambrose Bierce in *The Devil's Dictionary* (serialized 1881-1906; published 1906), without the bitter, brilliant, funny example of which there would be no *Idler's Glossary* and no *Wage Slave's Glossary*. See: CAPITALISM, WORK (REFUSAL OF)

LABOR (DIVISION OF) In any system where production is organized by private owners to maximize profits, a *division of labor* seems inevitable. Indeed, Adam Smith's *Wealth of Nations* (1776) proposed that the division of labor is crucial to the productive social organization of work. Precise division of labor facilitates the development of mechanized equipment to perform operations automatically, which in turn justifies further division of labor. But what are the implications for work when you substitute unskilled workers to do the simpler details of a job? The trend will always be toward the maximum use of unskilled (and therefore less highly paid) laborers; so more and more workers will labor at poorly paid, robot-like jobs. Only an elite few will get to conceptualize and execute their own work like humans. See: ALIENATION, KUDOKA

LABOR (EMOTIONAL) An implicit or explicit job requirement, identified by the sociologist Arlie Russell Hochschild, which demands that employees (often female, e.g., stewardesses, waitresses, nurses) strictly manage their internal feelings and express exaggerated or even false emotions. Recent research suggests that *emotional labor* may lead over time to employees' emotional exhaustion and burnout. See: BURNOUT, JOB SATISFACTION

LABOR (SPECIALIZATION OF) Specialization of labor leads almost inevitably to restricted power for workers. Why? Because managers and engineers must be hired to control the workers' behavior in a way that recoordinates their specialized activity. It's diabolical! See: BUREAUCRACY

LABOR (UNFREE) Work relations in which you are employed against your will (e.g., by the threat of destitution, detention, violence, or other hardship), and deprived of the right to leave, to refuse to labor, or to receive compensation in return. That is to say, nearly all work since the early 19th century – before which time work was organized in small-scale shops of independent artisans and their craft guilds and unions. Workers once controlled job training, planned production, and initiated improvements to the work process; today, they do what their managers demand. See: WAGE SLAVERY

LABOR (UNSKILLED) "When I was just a baby too little for the cotton sack/ I played in the dirt while the others worked/ 'Til they couldn't straighten their backs," ventriloquizes Johnny Cash in "I Never Picked Cotton." "And I made myself a promise when I was old enough to run/ That I'd never stay a single day in that Oklahoma sun." See: LABOR (DIVISION OF)

LAYOFF Originally, the term referred to a temporary interruption in work, due to (say) a factory's work cyclically falling off. Today it usually means the permanent elimination of a position;

the former meaning is now captured by the phrase "temporary layoff" (as heard in the theme song to the TV show *Good Times*). See: DOWN-SIZING, FIRED

LAYOFF SURVIVOR SICKNESS A syndrome diagnosed in the 1990s by David Noer, who observed that employees who remain after a layoff can experience symptoms similar to those experienced by survivors of other tragedies: e.g., shock, anger, anxiety, grief. See: LAYOFF

LEAVE 'EM NAKED TERMINATION Mean-spirited corporate jargon for a termination strategy in which a firm lays off employees without providing any protection, compensation benefits, or outplacement services. See: BENEFITS (EMPLOYEE), SACK (GETTING THE)

LEISURE SICKNESS A syndrome diagnosed by Dutch psychologists, in the early 2000s, the victims of which are more likely to report feeling ill during weekends and vacations than when working. It is hypothesized that the symptoms (e.g., migraines, aches and pains) may arise from stress experienced as a result of being unable to relax. See: ATTENTION (CONTINUOUS PARTIAL)

LOAF-DAY Mid-19th-c. US slang meaning "a day when no regular work is done." See: BANYAN DAY

 LOCKOUT A work stoppage that isn't a strike, because it's not the employees who refuse to work – instead, it's the employer who's preventing them from doing so. It's a tactic used to put pressure on a union, i.e., by reducing the number of its members who are working, or to prevent slowdowns or intermittent work stoppages. Today, the tactic is often used by the robber barons of pro sports, particularly NFL owners. See: SLOWDOWN

LOYALTY TIME A labor-rights NGO reported that when workers are expected to arrive before their shift in order to, e.g., prepare machines, unpaid, it's euphemistically called *loyalty time*. See: OVERTIME (REGULAR), REPARTIMIENTO

LUNCH HOUR Various studies indicate that in the US, in recent years, the so-called lunch hour has shrunk to half an hour or less. "I see more and more in our culture where being overworked is a badge of courage," an employment lawyer told *USA Today* in 2006. "It's a major mistake to let work encroach even further on this time. People really need a break." See: BREAK

MANAGEMENT (SCIENTIFIC) By the 1900s-10s, in the US, *scientific management* (which restricts the power of labor in the work process, freeing the worker from the burden of decisions about how to perform a job) had become a mass movement. Critics have described scientific management as the division of labor pushed to its logical extreme, with a consequent "de-skilling" of the worker and transformation of industrial work into menial, repetitive drudgery. But some historians argue that even when scientific management was implemented (the theory was far more popular in print than practice), it failed to transform the workplace in the way that Frederick Winslow Taylor had promised it would. Still, if you ask me, it's the thought ("Let's add an alienating dimension to mass-production manufacturing!") that counts. See: ALIENATION, TAYLORISM

MANAGEMENT BY WALKING AROUND This alienated and unintentionally hilarious Organizational Behavior term is defined to mean "communication and learning that occurs when managers take the initiative to systematically make contact with a large number of employees." See: MANAGER

MANAGER "Every day when I get home from work/ I feel so frustrated, the boss is a jerk," sings Todd Rundgren in "Bang the Drum All Day." "And I get my sticks and go out to the shed/ And I pound on that drum like it was the boss's head." See: BOSS, WORKPLACE DEMOCRACY

MANAGER (SEAGULL) Slang term meaning "a manager who flies in, makes a lot of noise, shits over everything, then leaves." See: MANAGER

MANAGING UPWARD *Managing upward*, or managing your manager, means subtly preventing your hierarchical superior from screwing up at his job, or interfering with your work. See: PETER PRINCIPLE

MAQUILADORA PROGRAM Derived from the Spanish for "the practice of millers charging 'a miller's portion' for processing other people's grain," the Maquiladora Program was launched by Mexico to address the problem of unemployment along the US border after the Bracero Program ended. Cheap labor and the passage of NAFTA in '94 made Mexican factories attractive to US businesses. Maquiladora workers are paid low wages for long hours; and Roberto Bolaño's novel *2666*, which chronicles the murders of maquiladora workers, doesn't make the program sound any better. See: BRACERO PROGRAM

 McJOB Popularized by Douglas Coupland's *Generation X,* this mid-1980s neologism describes an unstimulating, low-paid job with few prospects, particularly one created by the expansion of the service sector. (Want fries with that?) A song by the Replacements from the same era expresses frustration with McJobbers who actually seem to think they've got it pretty good: "'Sanitation expert' and a 'maintenance engineer'/ Garbage man, a janitor and you, my dear/ A real union 'flight attendant,' my oh my/ You ain't nothin' but a waitress in the sky." See: CAREER OPPORTUNITIES, WORK (PRECARIOUS)

MICROBOREDOM A neologism coined by the marketing department at Motorola, *microboredom* describes those brief idle moments – i.e., waiting for a traffic light to change – from which new mobile phone technology offers an escape. Ugh. See: LEISURE SICKNESS

MOBBING Workplace peer pressure – to the point of emotional abuse, bullying. The authors of a recent study of the subject tell us that *mobbing* is the creation of a hostile environment "in which one individual gathers others to willingly, or unwillingly, participate in continuous malevolent actions to force a person out of the workplace." Mobbing victims are usually intelligent, creative, loyal workers. See: EMPIRE BUILDING, OFFICE POLITICS

MOHAWK VALLEY FORMULA By the late 1930s, after a decade of militant working-class struggle and other popular activism, American workers finally enjoyed some of the rights that had been standard for decades in other industrialized countries. Because violent strikebreaking techniques were no longer effective, business interests published the "Mohawk Valley Formula," a set of guidelines for would-be strikebreakers, in the National Association of Manufacturers' *Labor Relations Bulletin*. The formula suggests discrediting union leaders, frightening the community, forming puppet associations of "loyal employees" to influence public debate, and so forth. See: STRIKE

MOIL Archaic term – now a British regionalism – meaning "to labor at a task that makes you wet or muddy." Found, for example, in the medieval phrase, "To toyle and moyle for worldly drosse."

NB: If flop sweat counts, then office workers *moil*, too. See: SWEAT

MOM BOMB Washington, D.C., neologism meaning "the effect of motherhood on the pay of female managers." According to the US Government Accounting Office, for every $1.00 earned by a male manager with children, a female manager with children earns just 79 cents. PS: The term is also slang for "a soccer mom's giant SUV." See: GLASS CEILING

MONDAY (BLUE) Antiquated slang term meaning "a Monday spent in dissipation and absence from work." It's also the title of one of the most influential post-punk singles of all time. Some of the lyrics from New Order's 1983 song – "Those who came before me/ Lived through their vocations/ From the past until completion/ They will turn away no more" – express what it was like for members of the Original Generation X (born 1954-63) to grow up in de-industrialized cities like Manchester, England. See: WORKWEEK

MONDAY (SAINT) A term first recorded in the mid-18th century, it was used with reference to the not infrequent practice among workmen of staying home from work on Monday as a consequence of drunkenness on the Sunday before – i.e., on their one day off. Some suggest that this was the origin of what we know as the two-day weekend. See: ABSENTEEISM, WEEKEND

MONDAYISH Originally a clergyman's complaint (first recorded in 1804) of lethargy or disinclination as a result of the work of Sunday, in this age of "weekend warriors" who never chill out for a moment on Saturday or Sunday, we all know the feeling. See: WEEKEND, WORKWEEK

 MR. BLOCK Ernest Riebe's comic strip of this title, which conveyed the Wobblies' attitude towards workers who lacked class-consciousness or who sympathized with reformist (as opposed to revolutionary) workers' movements, appeared in an Industrial Workers of the World newspaper in 1912-14. The block-headed titular character inspired Joe Hill's lyrics: "Oh, Mr. Block, you were born by mistake./ You take the cake./ You make me ache./ Tie a rock to your block and jump in the lake." See: WOBBLIES

MUCKAMUCK Wobbly lingo referring to bosses, management, and others in power. It is derived from Chinook jargon – that is, from the pidgin trade language of the Pacific Northwest. A variation on *muckamuck* is the phrase "high muckety-muck." See: BOSS, WOBBLIES

MULTITASKING Computer-ese for "executing a number of programs, or tasks concurrently." By the mid-1990s, computer programmers and other nerds were applying this term to the practice of sending emails while talking on the phone, and so forth. Today, *multitasking* is an epidemic with sometimes-fatal consequences: engineers in LA and Boston, for example, have crashed their trains while sending text messages. See: DOWNTIME, HURRY SICKNESS

NEED In 1763, the counter-Enlightenment French polemicist Simon-Nicholas Henri Linguet was the first to decry wage slavery (though he didn't coin the phrase), when he wrote: "What effective gain [has] the suppression of slavery brought [the laborer?] He is free, you say. Ah! That is his misfortune... [Laborers have] the most terrible, the most imperious of masters, that is, need.... They must therefore find someone to hire them, or die of hunger. Is that to be free?" Ambrose Bierce put it more succinctly, and cynically: "APPETITE, n. An instinct thoughtfully implanted by Providence as a solution to the labor question." See: WAGE SLAVERY

NINE-TO-FIVER A person who routinely works at the office between the hours of 9 a.m. and 5 p.m. What a way to make living! The phrase has been used pejoratively since its first recorded use, in 1955: "I swore then and there... that I would never be a nine-to-fiver," writes John Godley, 3rd Baron Kilbracken, in his autobiography. But you don't have to be an aristocrat to reject the *nine-to-fiver* lifestyle. In his "9-5ers Anthem," Aesop Rock raps: "We, the American working population/ hate the fact that eight hours a day/ is wasted on chasing the dream of someone that isn't us." See: WORKDAY (EIGHT-HOUR), WORKING STIFF

NO CALL, NO SHOW A particularly unprofessional form of absence from a service job, one that will swiftly result in suspension and perhaps even termination of employment. See: ABSENTEEISM, PROFESSIONALISM

 NOBBING IT Archaic slang meaning "to prosper and become independent thanks to one's wits, without hard physical exertion." Derived from *nob*, slang for "head." See: GRAFT

NOSEBAG (PUT ON THE) Vanishing slang phrase meaning "to eat hurriedly while at work." A more

recent slang phrase for eating while working is "Dining al Desko." See: HORSE, COLLAR (OUT OF)

OFFICE "The brain is a wonderful organ," quipped Robert Frost. "It starts working the moment you get up in the morning and does not stop until you get into the office." For the sensitive soul, the white-collar workplace is a torture chamber, where the soul dies slowly – by a thousand cuts. "Held like water in your shaking hands/ Are all the small defeats the day demands," laments an anti-wage-slavery song by the Weakerthans. "Ten to six and nine to five/ Trying, dying to survive." See: NINE-TO-FIVER

OFFICE (LIFESTYLE) During the dotcom era, when Internet startups had trouble recruiting talent, some offices added juice bars, gardens, nap rooms, and other "chillout zones" where employees could relax. Naturally, such zones became just another place to work. See: BRAINSTORMING

OFFICE POLITICS Writing about office politics in a 1956 sci-fi novel, John Wyndham wrote: "Many a young man's gifts are stunted by them." Together, *empire building* and *office politics* represent a syndemic – that is to

say, each syndrome magnifies the negative effects of the other. See: EMPIRE BUILDING, MOBBING

OFFICE RAGE Extreme workplace anger, as described in the song "Take This Job and Shove It," made popular by Johnny Paycheck in 1977. ("The line boss, he's a fool/ Got a brand new flat-top haircut/ Lord, he thinks he's cool/ One of these days, I'm gonna blow my top/ And that sucker, he's gonna pay.") PS: If you enjoy watching printers, copiers, and phones being smashed, search this phrase on YouTube. See: POSTAL (GOING)

OFFICE SPOUSE The phrase "office wife," meaning "a female secretary with whom a male executive has a close, but non-romantic relationship," has been around since the 1930s. Today, working women reject this expectation among men. (They did back then, too; Lynn Peril's *Swimming in the Steno Pool* quotes a secretary in 1941 saying, "The only thing the boss's wife need worry about... is that some day, in a fit of rage, the overworked secretary may slay the dear man.") These days, instead of reinventing the nature of work in such a fashion that neither men nor women any longer feel the need to couple up platonically at the office, we've settled for making the phrase gender-neutral. Now we're equally alienated! See: AIR FAMILY, SECRETARY'S DAY

OFFICING A term meaning "to perform office-related tasks, such as photocopying or faxing, 24 hours a day, anywhere." It was coined in the 1990s by Kinko's. See: PHONEMANCE

ONBOARDING Human Resources departments no longer content themselves with new hire orientation; their goal now is to minimize the time before new employees are "onboard," which in turn reduces new employee turnover. "Drilling new hires in the company's values and priorities," "instilling an optimistic attitude towards the company," "helping new hires identify with their employer" – all these bland HR euphemisms mean the same thing: "getting new recruits to drink the Kool-Aid." See: JOB EMBEDDEDNESS, PPCV

OUTSOURCING The contracting out of a business function previously performed in-house. Supporters claim that *outsourcing* brings down prices, which benefits everyone; critics claim that it's a union-busting stratagem leading to job displacement. See: KUDOKA

OUTWORK Mainstream economists point to the transition, during the 1860s, from *outwork* (decentralized production, done by unskilled workers in their homes or small workshops, of clothing and shoes; also called "sweating") to mechanized factory production, as evidence of a natural progression from less efficient to more efficient production methods. But was mechanization truly more efficient than outwork? Some economic historians have argued that the productivity increase of the period might instead (or also) be chalked up to employers' discovery of new methods – i.e., "speedups" and "stretchouts" – of forcing work out of laborers. See: EFFICIENCY, PIECEWORK

OVERTIME Time worked over and above a person's regular or set working hours. If it's injurious (as some have suggested) to divide time artificially, into working hours and leisure or free time, then prioritizing the former over the latter only adds insult to injury. NB: It's interesting that the first recorded use of the phrase ("Carpenters workyng their owre tymes and drynkyng tymes uppon the ffonte in the chappell") suggests that 16th-c. carpenters' workdays routinely ended with boozing. See: LOYALTY TIME

OVERTIME (REGULAR) When labor is in short supply, either due to a shortage of workers willing to work for the pay offered or else because a company hasn't hired enough workers, workers can either volunteer or be required to man *regular overtime* shifts. (As Luther Dixon and Al Smith's "Big Boss Man" puts it: "You got me working, boss man/ Working 'round the clock/ I want me a drink of water/ You won't let me stop.") Because of stress, anxiety, and lack of relaxation time, regularly working long hours puts us at greater risk for heart attacks and other circulatory diseases. See: LOYALTY TIME, REPARTIMIENTO, SABISU ZANGYO

OVERWORK "A dangerous disorder affecting high public functionaries who want to go fishing." That's the definition of the term found in Ambrose Bierce's *The Devil's Dictionary*. See: GULAOSI, LUNCH HOUR

PAI MA PI One of the first Chinese phrases that foreign execs learn, upon visiting China for business purposes, is this term that means "flattering those in a position of power." Literally, however, it means "stroking the horse's bottom." See: BROWN-NOSE

PARKINSON'S LAW "Work expands so as to fill the time available for its completion," quipped the British naval historian C. Northcote Parkinson, whose 1955 essay on what he called *Parkinson's Law* was inspired by his experience in the British Civil Service. Not to be confused with Hofstadter's Law, which states that "It always takes longer than you expect, even when you take into account Hofstadter's Law." See: PETER PRINCIPLE, SOCIAL LOAFING

PATTIN' LEATHER African-American slang from the 1930s, meaning "walking the streets [i.e., on shoe leather] looking for work." In 1957, Richard Lewis (of the Silhouettes), found a catchy new way to describe this activity: "After breakfast every day/ She throws the Want Ads right my way/ And never fails to say, 'Get a job./ Sha na na na, sha na na na.'" See: WALLABY (ON THE)

PAUL'S WORK A 17th-c. British slang phrase meaning "a badly done job, a mess." The term apparently derives from the fact that untrustworthy and incompetent men would hang out at St Paul's Cathedral looking to pick up temporary jobs. See: GIG

PERKS or PERQS Employee benefits of a discretionary nature – e.g., take-home vehicles, hotel stays, meal allowances, even profit sharing – are known as *perks* or *perqs*. They don't come without strings: the purpose of perks such as daycare or a dry cleaning allowance is to make working long hours more convenient for employees. As Blake (Alec Baldwin) puts it in David Mamet's *Glengarry Glen Ross*, "As you all know, first prize is a Cadillac El Dorado. Anyone wanna see second prize? Second prize is a set of steak knives. Third prize is you're fired." See: BENEFITS (EMPLOYEE)

PETER PRINCIPLE "In a hierarchy," claim Dr. Laurence J. Peter and Raymond Hull's 1969 book, *The Peter Principle*, "every employee tends to rise to his level of incompetence." Which is to say: members of a hierarchy tend to be promoted so long as they work competently, until eventually they are promoted to a position at which they are not competent. Peter's Corollary adds that actual work is only accomplished by those who have not yet reached their level of incompetence. See: BROUGH SOWERBY, MANAGING UPWARD

PHANTOM VIBRATION SYNDROME Also known as "vibranxiety," *phantom vibration syndrome* is a neurological condition in which a cellphone user over-incorporates non-vibratory sensations and at-tributes them to the idea that they're receiving a call (when they're not); it's also a manifestation of one's neurotic need to always be connected, 24/7. See: PHONEMANCE

PHONEMANCE A recent survey determined that the majority of small business owners hold their cell phones for more hours per day than they hold the hands of their loved ones. Not to worry, counseled a press release from the office supply retailer Staples: "While this new 'phonemance' phenome-non would seemingly have the potential to over-take family time, the increasing popularity of the 'virtual office' actually illustrates how technology is enabling small business owners to achieve both increased productivity and a better work-life balance." Um, OK. If you say so. See: OFFICING, WORK-LIFE BALANCE

PIE IN THE SKY This phrase first appears in a 1911 song by Wobblies activist Joe Hill. The song, which parodies the hymn "In the Sweet By and By," and which includes the lines, "Work and pray, live on hay,/ You'll get pie in the sky when you die," pokes fun at the Salvation Army – an organization seen as being more concerned with the condition of workers' souls than their stomachs. Got decent working conditions with good wages and benefits? Lucky you: that's known as "ham where I am." See: BENEFITS (EMPLOYEE), WOBBLIES

PIECEWORK A form of performance-related pay, where – regardless of time spent on the job – a worker is paid a fixed "piece rate" for each unit produced or action performed. As a common form of labor, *piecework* had its origins in the guild system during the mid-16th century, when master craftsmen would assign their apprentices work on pieces which could be performed at home. PS: in the mid-19th century, the practice of distributing garment assembly among lower-skilled and lower-paid workers came to be known as the "sweating system"; in Wobbly lingo, any job where the worker is paid not for her time but by the volume she produces, is known as *gyppo*. See: OUTWORK, SLOWDOWN

 PINK SLIP Dating to a 1915 pulp novel about baseball, or maybe earlier, the term refers to the apocryphal practice, by a personnel department, of including a discharge notice – presumably printed in triplicate, the employee receiving the copy on pink paper – in a pay

envelope. Note that archivists have located no actual *pink slips*. See: FIRED

PLANTATION The first wage labor contracts, recounts anthropologist David Graeber, were contracts for the rental of chattel slaves – whether in ancient Greece or Rome, or in the Malay or Swahili city states in the Indian ocean. Speaking of slavery and the modern workplace, the third-world historian C. L. R. James has demonstrated that most of the techniques of organization employed on factory workers during the industrial revolution were first developed on slave *plantations*; that is, the origins of industry and industrial capitalism were first evolved under slavery until they reached the point where labor's return was enough to keep the laborer alive. See: BOSS, WAGE LABOR

PLAYBOR A neologism referring to the increasingly blurred distinction between online play (specifically: participation in social networks) and labor. When you voluntarily share information about yourself and your desires, via Facebook or Twitter, and that information is then sold to marketing analysts, weren't you working? See: GRIND

POSTAL (GOING) In the 1995 movie *Clueless*, when the teenage Cher says, "My father's going to go postal on me," audiences everywhere immediately got the (tasteless) joke. From the mid-1980s through the mid-1990s, United States Postal Service workers shot and killed managers, fellow workers, and members of the police or general public at an average rate of approximately four incidents per year. Why? Critics have called the Postal Service "a treadmill of angry monotony... a minefield of festering grievances... a boot camp, where supervisors behave like drill sergeants." PS: The rate of workplace homicide is actually higher in retail. See: OFFICE RAGE, PARKINSON'S LAW

PPCV *Perceived Psychological Contract Violation* is a psychologists' construct that rates employees' feelings of disappointment arising from their belief that their organization has broken its work-related promises. Your PPCV rating is derived from how you answer the following questions, on a scale from one to seven: "(1) I feel a great deal of anger toward my organization; (2) I feel betrayed by my organization; (3) I feel that my organization has violated the contract between us; (4) I feel extremely frustrated by how I have been treated by my organization." See: ONBOARDING, PULSE SURVEYS

PRAIRIE DOGGING When someone working in a cube farm shouts, or makes a loud noise, and everyone stands up to peer over the tops of their cubicles, the scene is reminiscent of prairie dogs popping their heads out of their burrows. See: CUBE FARM

PRESENTEEISM Human Resources-speak meaning "the feeling that you must show up for work, even if you are too ill or exhausted to be productive – or even if you don't have enough work to do." This is the sort of thing criticized by the queercore band God is My Co-Pilot's snarky tune "Work is Love," e.g.: "My workplace is warm & comfortable./ My workmates are my friends./ Work gives structure to my time." See: BOREOUT

PRIGUISTICS Neologism coined by the French psychoanalyst Corinne Maier, meaning "the priggish linguistics of business euphemism." See: BUFFLING, INCENTIVIZE

PROFESSION (ADAM'S) In the first scene of *Hamlet*, a grave-digging clown comments that "gardeners, ditchers, and grave-makers… hold up Adam's profession." He's referring, of course, to Genesis 3:23, in which (after the Fall) God sends Adam "forth from the garden of Eden, to till the ground from whence he was taken." Per this myth, digging is the oldest profession; therefore, the clown claims, it is also the noblest. See: GRAFT, WORK (DRUDGE)

PROFESSIONALISM We tend to use this term admiringly, to refer to men and women who use expert or specialized knowledge in their work, whose work is of the highest quality, and who strictly and uncomplainingly adhere to the ethos of their trade even when it requires them to make personal sacrifices – because their honor is at stake. However, the greatest movie ever made about *professionalism*, Howard Hawks' *Red River* (1948), suggests to this viewer that one's motivation for getting the job done, no matter what the cost, isn't an ethos but a deep-rooted feeling of terror. See: FREELANCER

PROMOTION For white-collar workers, advancement within their organizational hierarchy is something about which they might spend nearly every waking moment fantasizing and scheming. When one's hopes for *promotion* are dashed, it's devastating; as, for example, in Edgar Lee Masters' poem "Clarence Fawcett,"

whose narrator reminisces mournfully from the grave: "The sudden death of Eugene Carman/ Put me in line to be promoted to fifty dollars a month,/ And I told my wife and children that night./ But it didn't come..." See: GLASS CEILING, PETER PRINCIPLE

PROUDHONISM Pierre-Joseph Proudhon's 1840 treatise, *What is Property*, answered that question with the immortal line "Property is theft." This mutualist philosopher sought not to end the ownership of property, but only to ban profit (e.g., for landowners and capitalists) without labor. Marx denounced Proudhon's pro-property views, and Lenin derided *Proudhonism* as "an unscientific, anti-Marxist trend in petty-bourgeois socialism." In the 1960s, however, Proudhon's theories helped inspire the *autogestion* movement in France; and Proudhon is today hailed as one of the most influential theorists of anarchism. See: AUTOGESTION, CAPITALISM He was also homophobic.

PULSE SURVEYS Large corporations, eager to find out how employees feel about the workplace without actually engaging directly with employees, are fond of attitude surveys with a scientific or even medical purview. One popular example is the HRRI Pulse Survey, designed by the Cen-

138

ter for Human Resources and Labor Studies "to measure the opinions or 'pulse' of an organization's employees in order to improve the organization's performance or 'health.'" The narrator of Ed Park's 2008 novel, *Personal Days*, describes the statements in one such attitude survey (e.g., "As the workday ends, it's OK to relax") as having "a North Korean vibe, affectless yet intense"; a colleague suggests there's a law against interrogation. See: HUMAN RESOURCES, JOB SATISFACTION

RAT RACE An early-20th-c. colloquialism meaning "a fierce competition to maintain or improve one's position in the workplace or social life." William Sloane Coffin, the Yale chaplain who became a leader in the civil rights and peace movements of the 1960s, warned undergrads: "Even if you win the rat race, you're still a rat." See: CAREER

REDUNDANCY The British equivalent of the US term *layoff*, meaning "termination of employment for business reasons." Same difference, really, though being "made redundant" somehow sounds – and perhaps also feels – worse than merely being laid off. See: DOWNSIZING, LAYOFF

REPARTIMIENTO A colonial forced labor system imposed by Spain upon the indigenous populations of its colonies. Though it wasn't technically slavery, the *repartimiento* forced workers to do low-paid or unpaid labor for a certain number of weeks or months each year on Spanish-owned farms, mines, workshops, and so forth. Ever been forced to work unpaid overtime? Then you know the feeling. See: CORVÉE, LOYALTY TIME

RETIREMENT Because few Baby Boomers will have the traditional pensions that many of their parents and grandparents had, and because members of Congress are pushing to scale back Social Security benefits (even though half the nation's retirees receive at least 90 percent of their income from Social Security), and because the financial crisis that began in 2008 caused 401(k) plans to tumble, some 45 percent of Boomers might not be able to maintain their living standards once they retire. For those of us now in our 20s, 30s, and 40s, retirement will be even worse. See: NEED You can't predict the future!

RETIREMENT (ACCIDENTAL) When an individual over the age of 50 in today's economy is laid off, she faces the prospect of aging out of the labor force before she's able to find another job. Hence the phrase *accidental retirement*, not to be confused with *funemployment*. See: GREYBEARDING

ROBOT Wilhelm von Humboldt argued that "whatever does not spring from a man's free choice… he does not perform it with truly human energies, but merely with mechanical exactness." This sort of classic liberal critique is at the heart of Czech litterateur Karel Čapek's 1921 play, *R.U.R.*, which introduced the coinage *robot* (from the Czech word for corvée) to describe android workers of the future. But surely it's also the point of L. Frank Baum's 1913 musical play, *The Tik-Tok Man of Oz*, the titular character of which sings: "Always work and never play/ Don't demand a cent of pay/ What I'm bound to do I do/ Isn't that the nicest way?" See: CORVÉE, FORDISM, WORKING STIFF

ROUSTABOUT "I'm just a roustabout/ Shiftin' from town to town/ No job can hold me down/ I'm just a knock-around guy…." So sings Elvis on the title track of *Roustabout* (1964). A *roustabout* [from the 18th-c. dialect term "rouze-about," a restless, roaming person] is an itinerant laborer picking up unskilled work on oil rigs, or in circuses. See: GIG, JOB PRECARIOUSNESS

SABISU ZANGYO Japanese for "uncompensated overtime." That is, work done off the clock because a superior or employer fails to compensate employees for, e.g., meal periods and rest breaks; time spent working while traveling; attendance at training, meetings and lectures; and so forth. In extreme cases, *sabisu zangyo* can lead to *karoshi* (death from overwork). See: LOYALTY TIME, OVERTIME

SACK (GETTING THE) In the 16th century, when a workman's services were no longer needed, he would be told to fetch the sack in which he stored his tools, pack them into it, and move on. The Beatles' "You Never Give Me Your Money" pulls off a neat bit of parallelism by juxtaposing the sad-sack couplet "Any jobber got the sack,/ Monday morning turning back" with an escapist couplet about packing up your stuff: "One sweet dream/ Pick up the bags and get in the limousine." See: FIRED, LABOR (UNSKILLED)

SALARY A fixed payment from an employer to an employee as compensation for agreed-upon outcomes. Wages are based on hours worked; a salary isn't. The term derives from the Roman word *salarium*, which links regular employment with salt – i.e., a soldier's pay

142

may have been used to purchase salt. But Pliny the Elder claims that in Rome the soldier's salary was actually paid in salt; in which case the expression "worth one's salt" would refer to salaried employees. See: WAGE

SALARY-SERF A term invented by Dan Wells, publisher of this *Glossary*, in order to warn young job-seekers that salaried employment, however prestigious, can entail more stress, longer hours, and fewer protections than working for a wage does. See: SALARY

SATURDAY "'Cause I'm up early in the mornin'/ Haulin' coal by dawn," sings Lee Dorsey in "Working in a Coalmine." Or at least that's what it sounds like he's singing. "But when Saturday goes around," he continues, "I'm too tired for havin' fun." See: WORKWEEK, WEEKEND

SCAB A laborer – whether a union member or not – who works during a strike. The term dates at least to 1777, when a worker in the British shoe-making industry wrote, of a recent strike, that "The Conflict would not been so sharp had not there been so many dirty Scabs; no Doubt but timely Notice will be taken of them." Centuries later, the term still stings. In Todd Solondz's 1998

143

black comedy, *Happiness*, when Joy Jordan (Jane Adams) is confronted by students whose striking teacher's job she's taken, she indignantly replies: "I am not a scab... I am a strikebreaker." See: BLACKLEG, STRIKE, UNION (TRADE OR LABOR)

SCULLION A male servant employed in a medieval household to do menial tasks, especially in a kitchen. The term *scullion* derives from a Middle English borrowing from an Old French word (*escouvillon*) meaning "little broom." A scullion is not to be confused with a scullery maid, who works in the scullery (washing-up, utility) room; the etymology of *scullery* is different – the term derives from the Latin *scutella* ("drinking bowl"). See: UNDERDRUDGE

SECRETARY'S DAY In 1952, the National Secretaries Association announced the first Secretaries' Week; its iconography focused on the secretary's boss-coddling duties. Alas, as Lynn Peril points out in her 2011 history, *Swimming in the Steno Pool*, the NSA "couldn't raise a woman's status in the mind of her employer or the public at large by promoting the profession as one of substitute wives and mothers who took care of men." Though it's now called Administrative Professional's Day, the pseudo-holiday's observance

(flowers, candy) suggests nothing has changed.
See: OFFICE SPOUSE

SELF-EMPLOYMENT The self-employed (sole proprietors, independent contractors, members of limited liability companies) are not wage slaves. This thought comforts us slightly as we contemplate working long hours, with unpaid overtime, for what often amounts to minimum wage or worse; and as we pay for our own health insurance and try to put something away for retirement. "Wrong life cannot be lived rightly," according to T.W. Adorno: that is to say, quitting your day job won't spring you from prison. See: BENEFITS (UNEMPLOYMENT), GETI JINGI

SHIFT (GRAVEYARD, LOBSTER) Working the *graveyard shift* originally meant working a lonely, and therefore dead-quiet, midnight-to-8 a.m. work shift... although it's more fun to think that the phrase might derive from the 18th- and 19th-c. fad of stationing a cemetery nightwatchman by the grave of a newly buried cholera victim, who (just in case he'd been buried prematurely) had been furnished with a bell to ring. In the 1920s, newspapermen working late at night were mockingly said to be on the *lobster shift*, either because lobsters are slow-moving, or because "lobster" was New York-ese for "fool," or else because the late-nighters were boiled (drunk). See: INEMURI

SICK BUILDING SYNDROME A syndrome consisting of non-specific, mild upper respiratory symptoms, headache and fatigue, experienced by occupants of older, relatively poorly maintained office buildings. The symptoms are generally attributed to temperature, humidity, and indoor air pollutants, but also to noise levels and flickering monitors. However, to an idler every office building is sick! The chorus of a lovely 1976 John Hartford song, for example, laments: "And it's goodbye to the sunshine, goodbye to the dew/ Goodbye to the flowers, and goodbye to you/ I'm off to the subway, I must not be late/ Going to work in tall buildings." See: BBS, WORK AVERSION DISORDER

SLACKOISIE This neologism describes "Generation Y" workers who (in the eyes of their elders, anyway) seem to view their job as an entitlement rather than a privilege, and complain about hours, benefits, and remuneration before they've earned the right to do so. Frankly, my sympathies are with the Gen-Y workers. See: DONE-DONE, FUNEMPLOYED

SLAVERY The abolitionist William Lloyd Garrison stated that the use of the phrase *wage slavery* (i.e., at a time when chattel slavery was still common) was an "abuse of language." He was right: being a wage slave is vastly preferable, in certain obvious ways, to being a slave. However, because it's more acceptable, to men and women of conscience, than chattel slavery, wage slavery is the more insidious threat. The historian E. P. Thompson notes that for British workers at the end of the 18th and beginning of the 19th centuries, the "gap in status between a 'servant,' a hired wage-laborer subject to the orders and discipline of the master, and an artisan, who might 'come and go' as he pleased, was wide enough for men to shed blood rather than allow themselves to be pushed from one side to the other." See: WAGE SLAVERY

SLOWDOWN or **SLOW WORK** Since the 1830s, piecework employees have responded to employers' lowering of the per-piece rate with a method of resistance known as the *slowdown* (also known as *soldiering*, or *pacing*). The idea is to maintain your pay rate at all costs. As an industrial action, a slowdown is a way to put pressure on management without striking – and therefore going unpaid. See: AUTONOMISM, PIECEWORK

SOCIAL LOAFING In 1913, the pioneering French social psychologist Max Ringelmann discovered the "Ringelmann effect": when he asked a group of men to pull on a rope, they did not put as much effort into the activity as they did when they were each pulling alone. Organizational Behavior researchers call this phenomenon *social loafing*, and theorize that it's one of the main reasons that workplace groups are sometimes less productive than the combined performance of their members working as individuals, i.e., because nobody is being evaluated individually. See: PARKINSON'S LAW, TEAM BUILDING

SOLDIERING Scientific Management guru Frederick W. Taylor spent a great deal of time in his books describing both individual and systematic *soldiering* (a.k.a. underworking, slow-working). Workers, he noted not unsympathetically, fear that increased output would lead to fewer workers; incentive schemes and hourly pay rates were not linked to productivity; and workers' rule-of-thumb processes were inefficient. Taylor was critical of management and labor alike; the former shouldn't drive the latter hard for low pay, while the latter shouldn't be lazy bums. PS: the term *soger* is archaic sailor's slang meaning "slacker, dodger, funker." See: SLOWDOWN, TAYLORISM

STAKHANOVITE The term derives from the name of Aleksei Grigoievich Stakhanov, a Soviet-era Russian *udarnik* (superproductive, enthusiastic laborer) who in 1935 supposedly mined 102 tons of coal in less than six hours – fourteen times his quota. A Stakhanovite movement, which looked both to Taylorist efficiencies and worker enthusiasm to increase labor productivity in the USSR, was born that same year; workers whose output exceeded quota were awarded recognition and privileges. In George Orwell's *Animal Farm* (1945), the workhorse Boxer is a Stakhanovite type, whose response to every problem is "I will work harder!" PS: After Stalin's death, it was revealed that Stakhanov hadn't actually mined all that coal. See: TAYLORISM, TEAM BUILDING

STOOGE *Stooge* is one of the greatest words in the American language; it's an early-20th-c. slang term meaning "work as an assistant or underling." The Three Stooges, a brilliant anti-wage-slavery vaudeville act, helped popularize the term for decades, from 1925 until Larry suffered a stroke in early

1970. Which, coincidentally, was just a few months after the release of The Stooges' self-titled first album. On it, Iggy Pop sings "I Wanna Be Your Dog," a proto-punk anthem of blue-collar alienation and self-abnegating lubricity. The torch had been passed! See: WORK ETHIC, WAGE SLAVERY

STOPPO Mid-century slang term meaning "escape, getaway," i.e., from a bank robbery or prison; in the 1930s, however, it had originally meant "a break from work." See: FLIGHT RISK, GRINDING HOUSE

STRESS Most solutions advanced to reduce stress address only its symptoms. Little is ever done to address the true source of the problem: work organization. Why research characteristics of the stressed-out individual (e.g., personality, genetics) when we ought instead to be negotiating more workplace control for laborers? See: ATTENTION (CONTINUOUS PARTIAL), MULTITASKING

STRESS INTERVIEW A job interview in which the applicant is purposely made uncomfortable, in order to assess her capacity for stress. Techniques include: *putting you on the spot*, *popping the balloon* ("Well, if that's the best answer you can give..."), and *doubting your veracity*. In 1997, the satirist Paul Maliszewski substituted a few words in a CIA torture manual and submitted the resulting document – which included tips on rendering employees more pliable via "unpatterned and aimless questioning sessions" – to a regional business journal. Naturally, it was published. See: PULSE SURVEYS

 STRIKE A concerted cessation of work on the part of workers, for the purpose of obtaining some concession from the employer. The term *strike*, used in this context, was first recorded in 1810; most western countries partially legalized striking in the late 19th or early 20th centuries. Though the strike is the unionized worker's principal economic weapon, some leftist critics argue that because skilled workers benefit more in both absolute and relative terms from striking than less skilled workers do, unionizing tends to redistribute wealth in an unfair manner. See: MOHAWK VALLEY FORMULA, SCAB

STRIKE (SERVILITY) In a 2011 Harper's essay, Thomas Frank called for a "twenty-four-hour refusal to fawn. A *servility strike*." Why? It would do nothing to alter the way our economic system "divvies up what we produce, suborns the state, sends your job to China, and smashes your retirement fund for good measure," Frank acknowledged. But at least it might make the "affluent louts" produced by that system less arrogant. See: REFUSAL TO WORK

SUNDOWNER In India during the British Raj, the type of vagabond who'd straggle into an upcountry station at fall of evening, pretending to look for work at an hour when he knew very well that work was ended for the day, was known as a *sundowner*. Note that in Douglas Adams' *The Meaning of Liff*, an *ozark* is the same type. See: *The Idler's Glossary*

SURVEILLANCE (WORKPLACE) Whether they're recording the websites that employees visit from their work computers, monitoring their email or telephone calls, or videotaping them at the water cooler, many businesses today are minding their employees' business. Though the argument for surveillance claims it creates a safer environment and prevents theft, most of us suspect that productivity is why we're being spied on. See: EYESERVICE

 SWEAT In late-19th-c. slang, to sweat was "to work very hard." In the 20th century, the slang phrases "sweating bird turds," "sweating bricks," and "sweating bullets" emerged. But now that we live in a postindustrial

society, sweat has developed a positive connotation: it's contemporary teenage slang for "like, love, appreciate." See: MOIL

SYNERGY A 1990s buzzword expressing the notion that corporate mergers will lead to efficiencies and financial benefits. In 1997, when the author of this *Glossary* worked at the start-up Web business Tripod.com, he pranked the producers of the TV newsmagazine show *Nightline* by rattling off ersatz digital newspeak: "Let's get FTP connectivity hyped up to the hilt. Let's get the synergies ramping." They ate it up. See: PRIGUISTICS

TAYLORISM Left-leaning social scientists (who believe that the organization of modern industry is inherently exploitative) have for decades made Taylorism a central feature of their critique of American capitalism. Frederick Winslow Taylor was an industrial engineer, and a leader in the Efficiency Movement of 1890-1932; his 1911 book, *Principles of Scientific Management*, helped influence the industrial world's shift away from skilled craftsmanship and piecework toward machine-tending which required little training or effort. Though the point of Taylorism is separating physical from mental labor, increasing the pace of work, and enhancing the manager's control of the worker, Taylor worried that his methods might be used "more or less as a club to drive the workmen into doing a larger day's work for approximately the same pay"; he'd hoped that they would instead be used for the mutual benefit of employer and employee. In a few rare cases – e.g., the Olivetti typewriter company under Adriano Olivetti – they were. See: EFFICIENCY, MANAGEMENT (SCIENTIFIC)

TEAM BUILDING Bonding exercises and more complex simulations and group-dynamic games aimed at improving a business team's communication, collaboration, and productivity. Ugh! The author of this *Glossary* so abhors such activities that he once wrote a satirical *team-building* exercise brochure for *The Baffler*, in which a group of businessmen are required to canoe down the Cahulawassee River in Georgia, endure a sexual assault from hillbillies, then fight their way back out. See: SOCIAL LOAFING, STAKHANOVITE Class· prejudice

TEDIUM Though it's not as overwhelmingly awful as boredom, much less ennui or spleen, the experience of *tedium* (Latin for "wearied, especially by monotony") is no fun. Repetitive work triggers it: in the song "Shove This Jay-Oh-Bee," from the *Office Space* soundtrack, Canibus raps: "Yo, six o'clock every morning you waking up yawning/

To the sound of your alarm clock alarm/ About an hour from now/ You should be at the place of employment/ Which is annoying cause it's so boring." Word. See: BOREOUT

TELECOMMUTING A work arrangement in which employees can choose their own working location and (to a lesser extent) their own hours. Work-at-home professionals work in their kitchens; nomad workers and web commuters work from coffeeshops, telework and remote office centers; freelancers and entrepreneurs might co-work and socialize in shared offices ("jellies"). *Telecommuting* is supposedly good for the environment, and a desirable perquisite for employees who hate commuting; the downside is that it can be difficult to leave work at the office every evening. See: AFTER-DINNER MAN, COWORKING, FLEXECUTIVE

TGIF A wage slave's acronym meaning "Thank God it's Friday." (Some snarky atheists would prefer that we use the acronym BGIM, meaning "Blame God It's Monday.") In the UK and Australia, workers sneaking out of the office early sometimes use the acronymic phrase "POETS Day," meaning "Piss Off Early Tomorrow's Saturday," or "Punch Out Early Tomorrow's Saturday." NB: In Hawaii, the phrase *Pau Hana* ("fin-

ished work") is used in the same circumstances.
See: WORKWEEK

THERBLIG A *therblig* is a fundamental unit of work
– e.g., looking, choosing, reaching, grasping, releasing – into which a manual operation or task
may be divided. The term, which is a semi-reversal
of their name, was coined by management consultants Frank and Lillian Gilbreth, who in the
1910s-20s invented the field of time and motion
study. Unlike fellow efficiency guru Frederick
Winslow Taylor, who sought to increase profits by
reducing process times, the Gilbreths sought to
decrease fatigue for workers by reducing the number of motions involved in their efforts. PS: As de-
tailed in the 1948 memoir *Cheaper by the Dozen*,
the Gilbreths often used their twelve children and
themselves as experimental guinea pigs. See:
EFFICIENCY, TAYLORISM

 TIME AND MOTION STUDY A scien-
tific-management procedure which
combines Frederick Winslow Taylor's time-study techniques with
Frank and Lillian Gilbreth's mo-
tion-study techniques, *time and motion studies*
were first instituted in US offices and factories in
the early 20th century. Workers complained that

the procedures benefited only the company, and adversely affected labor; the resulting job simplification not only led to tedium and boreout, but sometimes to decreases in pay and employment. See: EFFICIENCY, TAYLORISM, THERBLIG

TIME BIND In her 1997 study, *The Time Bind*, sociologist Arlie Russell Hochschild found that although working parents may believe that "family comes first," few take advantage of flextime, paternity leave, telecommuting, or other family-friendly policies offered by their employers. Home has become the new work (stressful, somewhere you don't want to be), and the office a refuge. Her suggestion: a parent-led "Time Movement," which would liberate us from work-driven tyranny. See: HOUR-GLASS CEILING

TRUCK SYSTEM An exploitative 18th- and 19th-c. arrangement in which employees were paid in company scrip (a substitute for legal-tender currency) rather than with money. Though ostensibly an example of free exchange, under the *truck system* (from the French *troquer*, meaning "exchange, barter"), workers usually had no choice but to redeem their scrip at high-priced company stores; this state of affairs was dramatized in the 1930s-era folk song "Sixteen Tons," in which a coal miner tells Saint Peter he can't go to Heaven because "I owe my soul to the company store." See: WAGE SLAVERY

UNDERDRUDGE The most menial of household positions; an *underdrudge* is a servant who reports to a servant. The British term *char*, which in the mid-18th century meant "one hired to do work by the day," later became a synonym for underdrudge. See: SCULLION

 UNEMPLOYMENT A permanent level of *unemployment*, such as exists in every western society, presupposes a population which is to a large extent dependent on a wage or salary for a living; and it presupposes the right of businesses to hire and fire employees in accordance with commercial or economic conditions. Prior to the capitalist era, except in the case of natural disasters and wars, unemployment on a large scale rarely existed. See: 99ERS, BENEFITS (UNEMPLOYMENT), HANG FIRE

UNION (TRADE or LABOR) An organization of workers banded together to achieve common goals, such as higher wages or improved working conditions. While craft unionism seeks to organize workers in a particular industry along the lines of their particular craft or trade, industrial unionism organizes all workers in the same industry into a single union. Some revolutionists lament that unions divide workers into competing factions, rather than organizing them as a single class. Also, it's been argued that trade or labor unionism is more useful to capitalists than to workers, as a kind of safety-valve that helps channel working-class discontent in a reformist, rather than revolutionary direction. The anarchist Mikhail Bakunin, for example, wrote in 1872 that "To me the flower of the proletariat is not, as it is to the Marxists, the upper layer, the aristocracy of labor, those who are the most cultured, who earn more and live more comfortably than all the other workers." See: STRIKE, WOBBLIES, WORKDAY (EIGHT-HOUR)

WAGE Compensation which workers receive in exchange for some quantity of their time; the word is derived from the Old French for "making a promise, e.g., in monetary form." Not to be confused with a salary, which is paid periodically without reference to a specified number of hours worked. "Earning a wage is a prison occupation/ and a wage-earner is a sort of gaol-bird," explains D.H. Lawrence. "Earning a salary is a prison overseer's job/ a gaoler instead of a gaol-bird." See: DUNG, FLINT, SALARY

WAGE (LIVING) In the 1870s, as the US was transformed into a wage labor society, workers and their unions increasingly abandoned their former hostility toward what they'd derided as "wage slavery" and began to demand a *living wage*. Which meant: sufficient wages to support families, maintain self-respect, and participate in civic life. Globalized supply chains have brought back a demand for living wages, by labor rights advocates; but multinational corporations have successfully argued that there is no internationally agreed-upon definition of any such thing. See: UNION (TRADE OR LABOR), WAGE LABOR

WAGE (MINIMUM) On their 1990 album, *Flood*, the band They Might Be Giants expresses outrage at the very notion of working for minimum wage via a minimalist song ("Minimum Wage") whose lyrics are as follows: "Minimum Wage. Heeya! [sound of cracking whip]" See: MCJOB

WAGE (RESERVATION) The *reservation wage* rate is the minimum wage rate at which a potential worker will accept employment. Because the worker's alternatives to paid employment (e.g., taking care of children, pursuing education, leisure) have positive value, the reservation rate is greater than zero. President Obama's former White House economic adviser Lawrence Summers claims that "government assistance programs contribute to long-term unemployment... by providing an incentive, and the means, not to work. Each unemployed person has a 'reservation wage' – the minimum wage he or she insists on getting before accepting a job." See: 99ERS, UNEMPLOYMENT

WAGE LABOR "That she should sleight me, and run away with a wages-fellow, that is but a petty Cleark and a Serving-man," marvels a snooty character in a 1641 play. It wasn't just aristocrats who regarded *wage labor* as no fit way to make one's living. In an 1847 pamphlet, Karl Marx wrote, "The slave, together with his labor-power, was sold to his owner once for all.... The [wage] laborer, on the other hand, sells his very self, and that by fractions. He auctions off eight, 10, 12, 15 hours of his life, one day like the next, to the highest bidder...." In the latter part of the 19th century, as the artisan tradition slowly disappeared, a few others began to agree: in 1869, The *New York Times* described wage labor as "a system of slavery as absolute if not as degrading as that which lately prevailed in the South." See: CAPITAL, SLAVERY, WAGE SLAVERY

WAGE SLAVERY Though similarities between chattel slavery and wage labor had already been noted by everyone from Cicero to Thomas Jefferson, 19th-c. textile workers in Lowell, Mass., were the first to use the phrase *wage slavery*. The Lowell Mill Girls, as they were known, condemned the "degradation and subordination" of the emerging industrial system; during their 1836 strike, one of their songs went: "Oh! isn't it a pity, such a pretty girl as I/ Should be sent to the factory to pine away and die?/ Oh! I cannot be a slave, I will not be a slave..." Their coinage called attention to the similarities between buying and renting a person; they denounced a social order in which you're encouraged to believe that you're free to direct your own life, when, in fact, you are dependent on income derived from wage labor. See: CORVÉE, SLAVERY, WAGE LABOR

WALLABY (ON THE) Australian slang term meaning "tramping the country on foot looking for work." Speaking of free-ranging Australian mammals, the word *dingo* is 1920s-30s Wobbly slang for "a tramp or hobo who refuses to work." See: PATTIN' LEATHER

WAYZGOOSE In the 17th century, a master-printer would throw his workmen a party on Bartholomew-tide (August 24), thus marking the end of summer and the shift to winter working, when candles were needed to light the final hours of the long working day. Though a goose might sometimes have been served at this feast, there is no known connection between the mysterious term *wayzgoose* and the fowl. See: BEANFEST OR BEANO

WEEKEND "Unions: The people who brought you the weekend." Those bumper stickers are telling the truth. But the weekend is a mixed blessing: in his 1991 history of the subject, the Canadian historian of ideas Witold Rybczynski notes that "the weekend has imposed a rigid schedule on our free time, which can result in a sense of urgency… that is at odds with relaxation." The rituals and protocols of the weekend are, for most of us, nothing (Rybczynski argues persuasively) but a "deceptive placebo" to counteract the exhaustion and boredom of the workweek. See: LEISURE SICKNESS, SATURDAY

WOBBLIES At its peak in the early 1920s, the Industrial Workers of the World (the *Wobblies*), who contended that all workers should be united as a class and that the wage system should be abolished, claimed some 100,000 members. Founded by socialists, anarchists, and radical trade unionists

163

opposed to the policies of the American Federation of Labor, the IWW's goal was to overthrow the employing class and usher in a new economic system that emphasized people over profit. See: MR. BLOCK, PIE IN THE SKY, UNIONISM (TRADE OR LABOR)

WORK "Work is a four-letter word," sings Cilla Black in the title song from the 1968 British comedy of that title. The plot revolves around David Warner's character's attempt to get a job for which he is over-qualified – tending the boiler room of the ultra-modern DICE Corp. – so that he can focus on doing the only thing he truly loves: growing psychedelic mushrooms. Like many supposedly counter-cultural films of the period (e.g., *What's So Bad About Feeling Good?*) the movie's message is actually counter-counter-cultural: Black wants Warner to shape up. See: *The Idler's Glossary*

WORK (DRUDGE) An early 16th-c. term meaning "the most unpleasant, uninspiring, monotonous kind of labor" – digging, in particular. For example, Robert Crowley's 1550 treatise, *An information and peticion*, which addresses the British Parliament on behalf of economically distressed commoners, contains the phrase "To tyll the grounde and doe your other droudgery." Eventually, the term *drudge* was applied to anyone employed in mean, servile, or distasteful work. See: GRAFT, PROFESSION (ADAM'S)

WORK (PRECARIOUS) Non-standard employment that is poorly paid, insecure, and unprotected – e.g., part-time work, self-employment, temporary work, on-call work, homeworking, and tele-commuting. Thanks to globalization, and the shift from a manufacturing to a service economy, *precarious work* is on the rise in the US. Women traditionally made up the majority of precarious workers; now that more and more men are being assigned such forms of employment, some pundits claim that work has been "feminized." It's more accurate to say that everyone is screwed. See: GIG, JOB PRECARIOUSNESS

WORK (REFUSAL OF) *The Right to Be Lazy* author Paul Lafargue, autonomists like Antonio Negri and Bifo, and post-left anarchists like Bob Black have at various times advocated what Bifo calls "the daily action of withdrawal from exploitation, of rejection of the obligation to produce surplus value" – behavior otherwise known as *refusal of work*. Adapting to regular employment means getting your mind right (as the prison warden in *Cool Hand Luke* puts it); so don't adapt to this disciplinary norm! See: AUTONOMISM, FORDISM

WORK (TEMPORARY) *Temporary* or *temp work* is a full- or part-time gig where the employee is expected to leave the employer within a certain period of time. Temps are never guaranteed consistent employment, and their assignments can end at any time. A "permatemp" is a worker classified as temporary who works alongside employees doing similar work at a business for a long period of time, though without receiving benefits. PS: College students who work at a job over their summer vacations are more accurately described as "contingent workers." See: GIG

WORK (WELFARE) Company towns, profit sharing, and other examples of *welfare work* (most often motivated by a vague altruism and benevolent control) were first developed in the 1880s; by the 1900s-10s, welfare work had become a mass movement. The most famous example of welfare work in action was a program – including the five-dollar day, and home visiting – introduced by the Ford Motor Company in 1913. Because Ford had simultaneously introduced a complex and easily disrupted mechanized assembly line, some business historians have argued that profit, not conscience, was the company's motivator for its sudden benevolence. See: FORDISM, PERKS

WORK AVERSION DISORDER A symptom of anxiety disorder, or a phobia. Sufferers work far less than is necessary in order to meet their monetary needs, even when opportunities exist to earn additional income; perform poorly at existing employment; or refuse to be gainfully employed at all, even when there are many potential jobs available. Not to be confused with idling, in which a person behaves in exactly the same way – but for reasons of existential health, not psychological illness. See: ABSENTEEISM, BURNOUT

WORK ETHIC Bertrand Russell claimed that it is the ruling class's "desire for comfortable idleness which is historically the source of the whole gospel of work. The last thing they have ever wished is that others should follow their [idle] example." In his 1989 anti-wage-slavery treatise, *Critique of Economic Reason*, the French economist and philosopher André Gorz decries the ideology of work, which assumes that: the more we work, the better off we'll be; those who work little or not at all aren't good members of the community; and those who do not succeed have only themselves to blame. This *work ethic*, Gorz insists, is now obsolete. See: *The Idler's Glossary*

WORK-LIFE BALANCE A much-discussed antidote to burnout, absenteeism, and stress-related illness, *work-life balance* is an Oprah Winfrey-esque amelioration. For a more reasonable solution to these social ills, cue George Michael and Andrew Ridgeley's "Wham Rap! (Enjoy What You Do)" from 1982: "DO! YOU! ENJOY WHAT YOU DO?/ IF NOT, JUST STOP!/ DON'T STAY THERE AND ROT!" See: BURNOUT, TIME BIND

WORK LIKE A TROJAN "I been a cabbie and a stock clerk/ and a soda fountain jock jerk/ and a manic mechanic on cars," sings Tom Waits in "I Can't Wait to Get Off Work." "'It's nice work if you can get it'/ Now, who the hell said it?" Maybe it was the Greeks who said it. As recorded in Virgil's *Aeneid* and Homer's *Iliad*, the Trojans were a hard-working, determined, industrious people. A fat lot of good it did them! See: GRIND

WORK RECONSTRUCTION This utopian phrase implies a broader social, economic, and political process than mere job redesign. Central to work reconstruction is the concept of employee influence on work process decisions. The preceding deconstruction implied here is Taylorism, scientific management, and perhaps the division of labor generally. See: SCIENTIFIC MANAGEMENT, TAYLORISM

WORKAHOLISM "It is hard to have a Southern overseer; it is worse to have a Northern one," wrote Henry David Thoreau. "But worst of all when you are the slave-driver of yourself." The 1968 coinage *workaholism* (the proper, medico-legal term is *ergomania*) would have us regard excessive devotion to work as a symptom of a disorder. See: HURRY SICKNESS, LEISURE SICKNESS

WORKBRICKLE The *OED* informs us that the mid-17th-c. British colloquialism *work-brittle* means "eager to work, industrious"; in the US, the term mutated into *workbrickle*, which as recently as the mid-20th century was still used in the Midwest and Appalachia: "I wouldn't exactly say he's lazy but he is right smart workbrickle." See: STAKHANOVITE

WORKDAY (EIGHT-HOUR) Before the eight-hour workday (or 40-hour work week) movement, the working day for industrial laborers could range from ten to sixteen hours. In 1817 the pioneering

169

Welsh socialist Robert Owen coined the slogan "Eight hours labour, Eight hours recreation, Eight hours rest." Demand for an eight-hour workday led to the Chartist movement and the organization of the earliest trade unions; in 1866, the International Workingmen's Association declared, "The legal limitation of the working day is a preliminary condition without which all further attempts at improvements and emancipation of the working class must prove abortive, and The Congress proposes eight hours as the legal limit of the working day." However, it wasn't until after years of agitation that the Fair Labor Standards Act of 1938 made the eight-hour day the norm for many working people in the US. See: EIGHT-HOUR DAY, NINE-TO-FIVER

WORKER (KNOWLEDGE) The new world of work, they told us in the 1990s, is that of the *knowledge worker*. Work was getting cleaner, less physically burdensome and dangerous, and better paying! Maybe, but even in rich capitalist countries only a fraction of the population gets to be scientists, engineers, artists, and financiers. The vast majority of our countrymen work in food prep or as service workers, customer service representatives, retail salespersons, cashiers, security guards, waitresses. As for the schoolteachers, factory workers, and mid-level managers, their unions are being busted and their work deskilled and mechanized. See: KUDOKA

 WORKING STIFF "Please don't talk to me about work," sings Lou Reed in the song of that title. "I'm up to my eyeballs in dirt/ With work, with work." The nine-to-fiver is frequently compared to a robot; but some prefer an undead zombie metaphor. "Don't wanna be a workin' stiff/ Lose my identity," protest The Ramones. "'Cause when it comes/ To workin' 9 to 5/ There ain't no place for me." See: NINE-TO-FIVER, ROBOT

WORKPLACE DEMOCRACY Companies characterized by high levels of employee engagement, principles-based rather than rules-based work relations, and a problem-solving approach to workplace conflict are said to exemplify *workplace democracy*. In such workplaces, management becomes a domain shared between managers and staff. So is this still wage slavery? A cynic might find a parallel in a 1963 Malcolm X speech: "If the master's house caught on fire, the house Negro would fight harder to put the blaze out than the master would. If the master got sick, the house Negro would say, 'What's the matter, boss, we sick?' WE sick! He identified himself with his master, more than his master identified with himself." See: WAGE SLAVERY

WORKWEEK "Welcome to the workin' week/ You gotta do it 'til you're through it, so you better get to it," sings Elvis Costello. Sell-out! Idlers prefer the anti-work stance of, say, the Mekons' 1979 song "Work All Week." Before collective bargaining and worker protection laws, American workers sometimes worked twelve to sixteen hours a day, six to seven days per week. (By contrast, hunter-gatherer societies typically worked two-and-a-half days per week, at around six hours per day.) Studies show that shorter workweeks actually increase productivity, because workers become healthier (more exercise, less stress) and happier. See: WEEKEND, WORKDAY (EIGHT-HOUR)

XEROX SUBSIDY Euphemism for using the photocopier at work, for making one's own copies. Speaking from experience, I can attest that the zine revolution of the 1980s wouldn't have been possible without such a generous (if unwitting) subsidy. See: *The Idler's Glossary*

YAKUZA This pejorative moniker, embraced today by members of Japanese organized crime syndicates, dates to the mid-Edo period, when itinerant and heavily tattooed social outcasts made their living playing games of chance. *Ya-ku-za* (or 8-9-3) is a losing hand in the card game Oicho-Kabu, a form of blackjack; to be a yakuza, then, in a highly stratified social order, was to be an ostentatiously "useless individual." See: BEE (BUSY AS A)

ZERO DRAG A 1999 *New York Times* article noted that this term – borrowed from physics, and meaning "an ideal state where a moving object experiences no resistance" – had become New Economy slang for "a no-spouse, no-children way of life." Start-ups and other firms are often eager to hire employees whose drag coefficient is zero. If this way of life sounds attractive, just remember what Steve McQueen's character, Vin, in *The Magnificent Seven*, says about the nomadic gunslingers' way of life: "Home—none. Wife—none. Kids—none. Prospects—zero." See: JOB EMBEDDEDNESS, WORK-LIFE BALANCE

 **Joshua Glenn** is a Boston-based writer, editor, and cultural semiotics analyst. He co-founded the blogs HiLobrow and Semionaut; in the 1990s he published the zine/journal *Hermenaut*. He has labored as a barrel-washer and bartender, handyman and housepainter, skateboard courier and substitute teacher. He's worked 9-to-5 as an editor at *Utne Reader* and *The Boston Globe*. His previous book, co-authored with Mark Kingwell and illustrated by Seth, is *The Idler's Glossary*.

 After some years of graduate education in Britain and the United States, **Mark Kingwell** found he had inadvertently perfected a form of idling for which he could get paid. He is Professor of Philosophy at the University of Toronto and a contributing editor of *Harper's Magazine*, and has written for publications ranging from *Adbusters* and the *New York Times* to the *Journal of Philosophy* and *Auto Racing Digest*. Among his fifteen books of political and cultural theory are the national bestsellers *Better Living* (1998), *The World We Want* (2000), *Concrete Reveries* (2008), and *Glenn Gould* (2009). In order to secure financing for their continued indulgence he has also written about his various hobbies, including fishing, baseball, cocktails, and contemporary art.

 Seth is a cartoonist and designer. His books include *George Sprott*, *Wimbledon Green*, and *Palookaville*. He is the designer for *The Complete Peanuts* and the *John Stanley Library* and *Doug Wright, Canada's Master Cartoonist*. His latest book is *The Great Northern Brotherhood of Canadian Cartoonists*. In 2012 he will be designing a special 50th anniversary edition of Stephen Leacock's *Sunshine Sketches of a Little Town*. He lives by the railroad bridge in Guelph, Ontario with his wife and two cats.

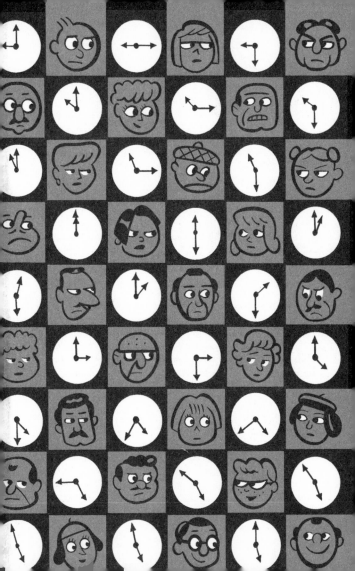

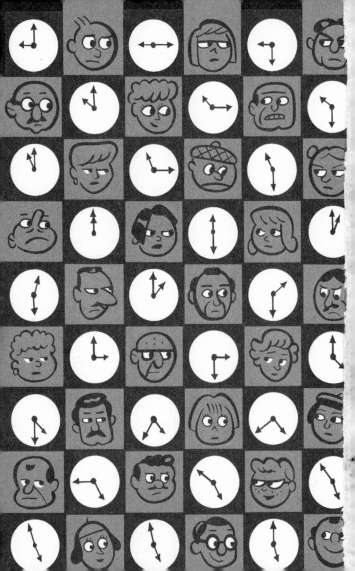